Reckoning 8
Electronic Edition: Winter 2024
Print Edition: Summer 2024

Cover and interior ornament by Martins Deep

Reckoning Press
206 East Flint Street
Lake Orion, MI 48362
www.reckoning.press
distributed by IngramSpark

 ISSN 2474-7327
e-ISBN 978-1-955360-10-4
ISBN 978-1-955360-11-1

Reckoning 8

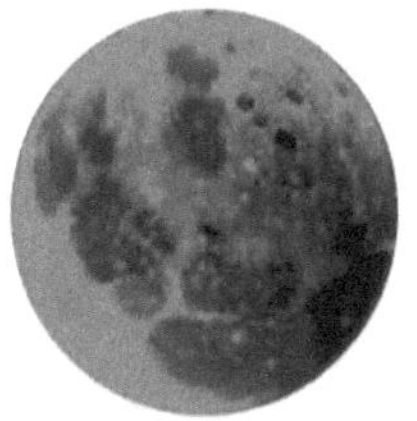

Contents

Cover:
Breaking Points

Martins Deep

Martins Deep (he/him) is a poet of Urhobo heritage, as well as a photographer and digital artist. Currently an undergraduate at Ahmadu Bello University, Zaria, his recent works have graced the pages of *Anathema Magazine*, *Josephine Quarterly*, *Native Skin Magazine*, *Paper Lanterns*, *Chestnut Review*, and more. He says hi @martinsdeep1.

From the Editors

Waverly SM

Early this year, when I was living in Canada and nobody was talking about Palestine, the Reckoning editors and readers decided we wanted to craft an issue about "all of this." We wanted work that dealt with active resistance, with intersecting oppressions, with opposition to the creep of fascism. I think we had a feeling it was going to get worse. I don't think we quite expected how.

Now, as I write this, I am about to move to the United States. I'm going to marry my fiancé, a trans man, and hopefully embark on my own non-binary transition. I'm about to be subject to systems I have never been subject to before, at a time when the future for people like us has never felt more uncertain.

Now we are watching the beginnings of a genocide in the Middle East, with no sense for how or when it will end. Palestinians are dying in droves. My Jewish friends and loved ones are outraged and furious and afraid.

Now every other month breaks a new temperature record. Now children are in court suing governments and states over the future they expect to inherit. Now we are staring down the barrel of an election year. Now this terror is just the way we live.

I wanted this issue to speak to that terror, without yielding to it; to acknowledge cruelty without denying complexity, and to reflect the moment without accepting it quietly. I wanted work that spoke to the instability of the world we have built, but also its mutability—and the ways we have it in ourselves to shape it.

We're in this, sure. There may not be an easy route out of it. But we're in it together, and we have the advantage of numbers.

I hope we've succeeded. I hope we will succeed.

I hope, full stop.

October 30, 2023
Rugby, England

Waverly SM is a 2019 Lambda Literary Fellow whose work has appeared in *We're Here: The Best Queer Speculative Fiction 2020* (Neon Hemlock, 2021), *Stim: An Autistic Anthology* (Unbound, 2020), *Lucent Dreaming*, *SAND*, and *Catapult*. They can currently be found trying to approximate the anchorite lifestyle on the unceded territory of the Ramaytush Ohlone People.

From the Editors

Knar Gavin

The question, as a form, courts: wide-spanning and invitational, it provides the grounds for voicing provisional answers and desires, variously. The works that comprise this issue of Reckoning provoke essential questions for our current historical conjuncture, questions which defy the treacherous narrows of business-as-usual and open instead toward livable futures at once wily and strange—futures filled with the surprises that come of persistence, of life-thrum, prevailing in spite of everything.

How are we to "link fingers in the dark" (following Kelsey Day); what do we do at the checkpoints, when everything goes wrong (querying after Joanna Streetly)? How do we carry the ravages of the past into urgent articulation with our planetary present? What does that carriage—of word and idea; of nightmare-begotten dreams—look like and hold? Where do its lines break, and what wastelands can it be machined into navigating? How do we multiply the tongues of refutation and ignite material practices that collectivize, that make places built against destruction and for flourishing?

Alongside my fellow readers and editors, I have sought, in this issue, to bring together writing that provokes such lines of questioning. In turn, the writers included here have helped me to ask and re-ask the question of militancy, and what it might—or ought—look like on the page.

I tend to agree with the great documentarian, Muriel Rukeyser: we must "walk in the river of crisis toward the real." Yet a profound recalibration of pace is in order. Amidst the ongoing genocide of Palestinian peoples, we must run, together, gathering the truth up in our hands and hurling it against the barricades to thought itself, which the state of Israel—backed by the death-fund of US empire—has thrown up to obscure the reality of this gruesome moment of flagrant, unblushing human sacrifice.

From Palestine to the abysmal failure of climate talks at COP28, the planet is ablaze with injustice. Even so, in the face of the anti-life operations of empire, menacing extractivism, and the killing racial logics of global capitalism, other stories *are* bursting forth; sites of resistance are erupting and lines of solidarity are being forged. I am grateful that *Reckoning 8* houses some of these stories—counter-behemoths to the fire-spiting behemoths of the now, which would render land, lives, and languages alike moribund (per Oluwatomiwa Ajeigbe's conjurings).

This issue insists that we can, indeed, must, be fierce and uncompromising, on *and* off the page. That we must retain and seize the right to dissent from planetary collapse, enacting, instead, the inevitability of resistance, that dear and dearly fruiting tree, its luminous stones sweetly enfleshed with fuel for the hurling.

December 27, 2023
Occupied Lenape Territory of so-called Philadelphia, Pennsylvania

Knar Gavin (they/any) is a doctoral candidate at the University of Pennsylvania, where they recently served as the Poetic Practice Fellow. Their research attends to representations of environmental crisis in late-20th- and 21st-century poetry and poetics, and they are drawn toward learning from and sharing the prefigurative political possibilities that emerge in works of documentary and ecopoetry. Knar is also an environmental justice organizer and participates in bottom-up collective struggles, including those against extractive, toxic industries and ecocidal development projects. Recent poetry can be found in *AGNI, NiCHE, Perpetual Doom*, and *West Branch,* and their 2019 poetry chapbook *Vela.* is available through the Operating System. You can find their essay on the idiom of "climate grief" in *Annulet: A Journal of Poetics.*

sunday in Atlanta

a poem

kelsey day

we walk, many legged, into the green.
pine needles sigh underfoot.

we sit on a blanket, bumblebees
drowsing on our laps. a
stranger makes us espresso,
presses brown sugar into a
tiny mug with a spoon.

then, the marshes flinch
back. the blue Road goes
tense. helicopters multiply
like acne overhead,
the sound a bloody thrumming.

(6)

we pull our bodies out of the Ground. music is playing. A bouncy house billows open, & the grown-ups take their shoes off.

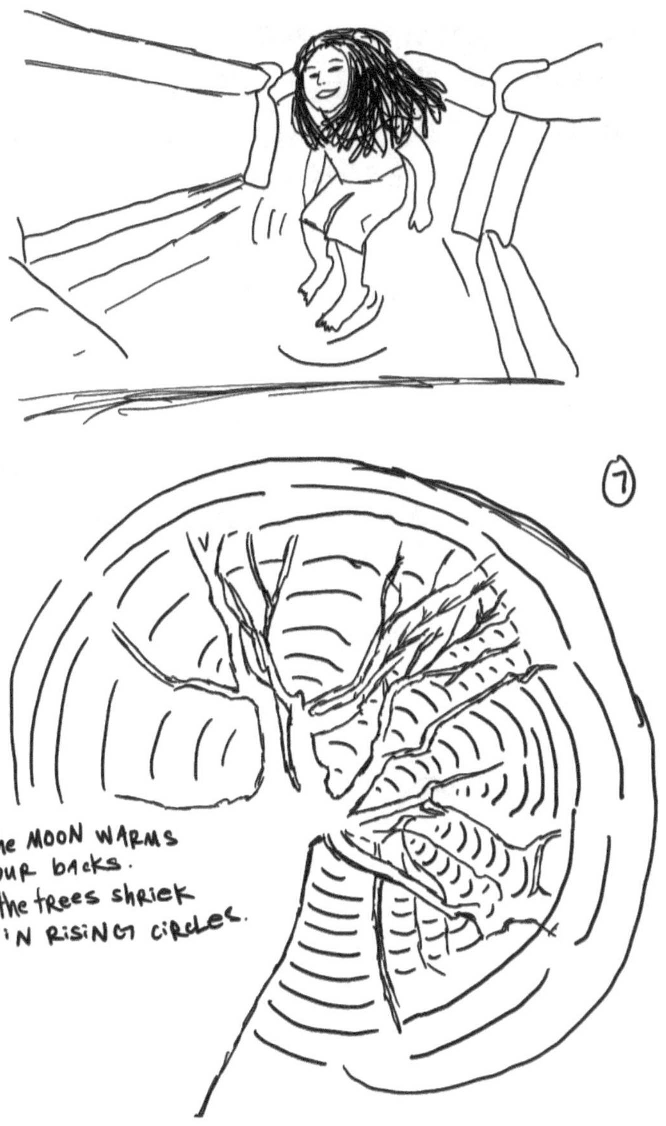

ACROSS CAMP, FIRE SPROUTS OVER METAL, LICKS WIDE, JAW OPEN. (8)

A COP POINTS A GUN AT THE BOUNCY HOUSE.

(10)

we CRAWL into the cracks, the bramble,
and wait.

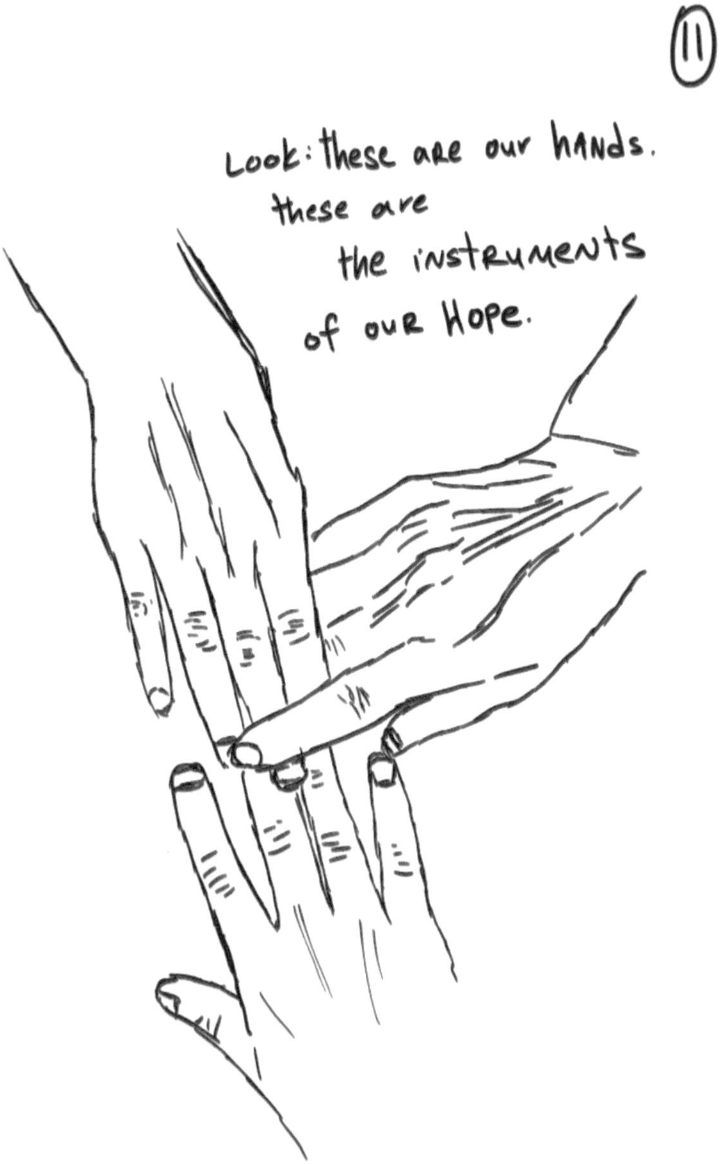

Look: these are our hands.
these are
the instruments
of our Hope.

this is
a cold, round
rock we pulled
from the river.
12
this is the oak that will
not fall.
13

this is the
vine that
wraps around
tight, & does
not let go.
14
this is the petal
that will not
be named

15

THIS IS OUR HOLY REFUSAL.
THIS IS THE BODY
THAT WILL NOT KNEEL.

COP CITY
WILL NEVER
BE BUILT.

17

Kelsey Day is a queer poet from southern Appalachia. Their work can be found in *Freeman's, The Appalachian Review, Washington Square Review, The Foundationalist, Brave Voices*, and *Our Shared Memory Collective*, and has been nominated for the Pushcart Prize, the Penrose Poetry Prize, and Best of the Net.

The X That Means Both Death and Life

Ariadne Starling

This story begins and ends with the X that means both death and hope.

Three Xs, two strikes, one message: Solidarity.

26 November, 2017.

The Australian government would prefer that we forget this crime against humanity, this X in flesh in the air.

It's a humid, sweaty, overcast day at a protest at Federation Square in the centre of Melbourne. Shen Narayanasamy of the progressive activist group GetUp! tells us that the police are beating with batons the refugee men who have spent 21 days in peaceful protest against their detention on Manus Island, Australia's refugee detention centre in Papua New Guinea. SHAME read the signs in the square. FOUR YEARS TOO LONG. *We're doing this today at the request of the men, to rise to the dignity of their example.* Natasha Blucher of the Asylum Seeker Resource Centre tells us whistleblowers' accounts of the Nauru camp, another offshore Australian refugee detention centre. *Amazing locals put themselves at risk to get us, journalists, food, and water into the camp.* The smell: There was two weeks' worth of garbage that the men had tried to collect and contain. Pulling water from a well with an oily film on top. Ingenious fresh-water catchment, bed sheets tied up with bottles at the bottom. Every cubicle in the toilets was full to the brim with diarrhoea. The men were so sick and had serious illnesses from three or four years locked up. Even in that toxic place, the refugees' culture of hospitality prevailed. *We ate biscuits that somebody had baked in the middle of a siege. They brought tea for us and added sugar. They'd saved it for guests.* HUMAN RIGHTS ABUSE A CRIME spake the signs. STOP VILIFYING REFUGEES. In the crowd I see Hijabi Muslim women of colour, young white guys in shorts, and many seniors holding photos of the refugees who have died in Australian camps.

There have been 14 known refugee deaths in offshore detention since 2014, including 7 by suicide. Senior women with purple shirts saying *Grandmothers against children in detention.*

The crowd is asked to kneel, or sit if we can't kneel, for four minutes, with our hands crossed above our heads, which is the way that the men of Manus had been protesting for 21 days. We squat or sit with difficulty for four minutes, hearing the words of Kurdish-Iranian asylum seeker Behrouz Boochani's statement, his dignity, his gratitude for our support. There is the hideous dissonance of a *Wallace & Gromit* exhibition ad in huge letters behind the crowd squatting with their hands crossed. The ad silently blares *It's hard to wipe the smile off your face!* Behrooz's statement is haunting: despite having not enough food themselves, the refugees had been feeding their dogs, and the police had killed one out of spite.

The sun breaks through the clouds and is thanked for it by a grateful speaker. Activists who used to teach at Victoria University speak with admiration of their migrant and refugee students' resourcefulness. The small moments of humour are some of the most striking. Leading us in the squat, a speaker says *It's okay to sit if you can't squat, if your knees aren't, you know, pilates.* The crowd chuckles, and I think about those small moments of levity, not because we're having fun, but because we recognise our shared humanity, our vulnerability.

This X is in flesh in the air, arms crossed in solidarity, the X of the refugee men's arms iconic of their captivity. The X that represents the deaths from which they flee and to which our policies have driven them. But their X is the hope of protest too, of shackles to be broken, and ours a tribute to their dignity and their deep humanity, unassailable.

Australia's federal government would prefer that we forget this crime against humanity, this X in flesh in the air. Will you let them?

13 November, 2019.

This X is the target that Aboriginal people have had on them in this colonised country for over 230 years. It is the X in the scope of a gun, too often turned on Black men, women, and gender-diverse people by police in this colony.

It is a grey day at the snap rally Justice for Kumanjayi Walker, a 19-year-old Warlpiri Aboriginal man who was shot by police in his home in Yuendumu, 300 km north-west of Alice Springs, in central Australia, on Saturday 9 November, 2019. A crowd begins to gather at the intersection of Bourke and Elizabeth Streets. A man with a sad expression, lines on his forehead, and a streak of rich red hair licking up from the right of his forehead addresses a circle of orange-and-yellow high-vis supporters. No microphone, but I see him mouth *They say it'll be a rally in the rain, well it'll rain. Those of you who've done this before…* A fat Black man with a clipped beard and red Indigenous-design dots across a red sports-style vest leans his face into the chest and over the left shoulder of a thin man in front of him, taking comfort from him. Two little Black girls huddle together under their Aboriginal flag to protect them from the beginning rain. A sign rises over the crowd. THE FUTURE IS BLACK. A chill wind blows down Elizabeth St and through the pillars I stand between at the top of the Bourke St post office steps.

The signs are heartbreaking. I see women looking desolate under hand-written and printed signs KILLED IN CUSTODY, the red and yellow letters stark against the black background. A fierce, articulate Black man gestures with his right hand as a bank of cameras point at him, *Terra Nullius is a legal fiction!* (*Terra Nullius*, Latin for "nobody's land," was the legal principle used by British settler-colonists to justify stealing the territory of Australia from its Aboriginal Traditional Owners during British colonisation in the late eighteenth century.) A woman with short white hair nods during the speeches, an Aboriginal flag rises above the lowered zip of her open black hoodie. Her mouth wobbles, she bends her head down to her left hand to wipe a tear, never putting down her sign *End the brutality! Stop the killings! Justice for Wayne!* Her stricken face resonates between the placards and I can't look away from her grief. The sacred smoke of burning eucalyptus leaves rises over the crowd in a wind that blows down Bourke St. An Aboriginal Elder raises his voice and a smooth dark brown staff and projects to us his name and his Country, and that he is from the Stolen Generations. He raises his hands to the sky and describes the spirits he is connected with—*I have been blessed*. A ripped cardboard sign rises before me, BLACK LIVES MATTER with strong strokes in yellow and red. The crowd has swelled and fills the tram tracks. I see the kind eyes of Aunty Tanya Day smiling from a poster.

Jaeden Williams, a Yalukit Willam man of the Boon Wurrung people, speaks. *My family have been here for 4,000 generations, for 100,000 years. This land has a story that is a lot longer than 150 years. According to the Boon Wurrung, this land was created by Bunjil, who travels as an eagle. He taught us to welcome all friends and guests. Bunjil's Laws are two promises, and these promises have been the essence of the land since time began.* He asks the crowd to speak after him, and we join our voices to say,

We promise
to look after the land
and the water
and we promise
to look after the children

That's been the spirit of this land, of Melbourne, of my culture, since time began.

A sign, white text on a black background:

16 . 03 . 2019
Veronica Baxter 34
IDENTIFIED AS A WOMAN
THROWN IN A MALE PRISON
FOUND HANGING IN CELL

Does anyone have clapsticks? asks a speaker. The powerful Elder raises his staff and says, *I've got a weapon of mass destruction!* and the crowd laughs along with him. A woman speaker asks us to put a hand over our hearts—*Breath in from our ancestors.* The crowd is silent, stricken faces, the pulse-pulse of our hands tapping a heart-beat on the cloth over our hearts. After finishing, *I think our ancestors heard us.* A tram leaves the intersection toward Queen St.

A speaker reads statements from Elders in the area, later published in *The Saturday Paper*.

From Marly Wells Naparngardi, a Warlpiri woman: *We came on Sunday morning to stand together in our grief and were presented with smirking police officers and no answers. Two mounted police attempted to bring their horses closer, an intimidation tactic. Someone requested them to leave and I heard one of the officers say, "If you had any respect for the horse's life you would stop waving the cardboard in its face. He doesn't like it. You're intimidating him." If you had any respect for human beings, if you had any respect for the Traditional Owners of this land, if you had any respect at all, you would be questioning the systems in place—the systems you benefit from, the systems that keep Aboriginal people down.* "SHAME!" breaks out and spreads across the crowd.

A person of colour in a white knit jumper and navy headscarf holds a sign spray-painted on the back, beneath three inverted triangles in the queer anarchist movement's pink and black,

QUEERS
AGAINST
COLONIAL
-ISM!

A man sings a Warlpiri song, a sad melody, and translates after every line—*He's missing his kids.* Signs are held over heads as the rain begins. *Police must not investigate police!* A woman with a rainbow beanie asks to take a little boy with pale short hair past me down the steps to see the speakers. The crowd cheers a speaker and the boy turns around in his bright giraffe-print coat to give her the thumbs-up. The boy explains to her that he's giving the thumbs-up to the speakers when the crowd claps to show his support. *Use of bush medicine, cultural practices, and Law.* Between speakers, a quiet descends over the crowd. A baby cries to my left and a motor idles on Elizabeth St.

The wind changes direction and blows up the steps towards me and I smell the sacred smoke of the eucalyptus. The women behind me are trying to find their friends in the crowd. "He's running." "Is he a super fitness nut?" The march begins and I join the back of the crowd and remember the enthusiasm and solidarity. A man and woman's voices begin the chant behind me, *Too many coppers: Not enough justice!* A person with short hair and intricate spiderweb and flower tattoos emerging from their sleeves holds a sign lettered in black, yellow, and red,

TELL
THE

TRUTH

The red of TRUTH drips in the rain down their left wrist off the bottom of the sign, ominous. *Too many coppers!* begins the chant and breaks off into giggles as *Too many coppers!* rolls back from the front of the crowd and confuses the rhythm. We cross Swanston St and bank up, the roar of the crowd swells. A Black woman with short black curls holding her takeaway dinner with a tiny sauce tub on top rests on a short plinth and smiles, and I recognise her expression—gratitude and pride.

19 . 11 . 2004
MULRUNJI 36
DIED IN CELL WITHOUT TREATMENT

Too many cop-pers! Not enough—the crowd breaks off and a woman in yellow next to me adds hesitantly, *Justice?*

The crowd banks and turns to the left and a woman behind me asks, *Are we stopping here?* and it's because there is a line of police in yellow high-vis in front of the Melbourne East Police Station, the letters of the sign booming towards us in 3D. I realise that the high-vis people I saw at the beginning are there to physically stand between us and the police, to protect us from their potential violence. Our guardians. They wear paper gas masks loose at the side of their necks, just in case, water bottles in their backpacks. The police watch uncomfortably.

We cross Russell St and a woman walking a shopping trolley and carrying a silver walking stick pipes up *No justice, no peace!* as she walks through the intersection. A woman with braids in a short, fluffy, red-lined jumper wheels her wheelchair with the march in front of us. I see two Eureka flags and the Torres Strait Islands flag flicking in the wind of the intersection ahead. A woman with a cane has an Aldi shopping bag and thongs—her feet look cold! She turns and laughs at her friend, a generous smile that rises from her cheeks under ginger bangs and hair trailing her shoulders and spilling out of a knitted beanie. A man with a sign, "Do ya want some water, Schazz?" "Yes please." A silver-haired man in a red beanie and a worn leather jacket with a small gum branch tucked over his ear grins and embraces a friend. I see the two rows of guardians bringing up the rear of our march. Water trickles down the tram tracks. I see the boy with the giraffe-print jacket in fluoro pink gumboots at the edge of the crowd.

The crowd banks up at the Parliament steps.

In 2017, Aunty Tanya Day fell asleep on a train after drinking and was woken up and arrested by police under an archaic law for public drunkenness that has been historically disproportionately used to incarcerate Aboriginal people. During her four hours in a cell, she fell and injured her head, unsupervised. When she was discovered, it took an ambulance one hour to arrive. She never awoke and died in hospital.

At the protest, Tanya's daughter Apryl Watson speaks, her voice struggling from the emotion: *We've seen again and again deaths in custody, straight-up murder.* Her voice is exhausted. *Can you tell me how many people went to the Melbourne Cup, got blind drunk—How many whitefellas died in a cell? How many white women had ambulances? They didn't give a shit about mum.* Her voice breaks down at the end of her line. *I've got my daughter at home, I can't even have her sitting next to me when I get breathalysed, she's crying because she doesn't know what's gonna happen to me, because she knows what happened to mum.*

The sinking sun illuminates the stone-faced pillars and the tiny gold sphere is a dot in the inscrutable sunglassed eyes of every cop on the steps of Parliament.

We hear the righteous anger of a speaker. *12 years ago my nephew was found handcuffed in an alley and do you think anything happened to them police? The look of 'em, looking at us like we're dickheads. They're racists, they're murderers! Every year this is happening! This Victorian government here was the first Constitution—Terra Nullius began here. If we had sovereignty recognised in this country, would we be in their jails? Would they be stealing our children?* His voice rises to a sharp growl. *They don't give a fuck about us!*

A line of Black women at the front hold up red-painted palms to the police line as we in the crowd chant *Blood on your hands!* Apryl Watson, her palms reddened, wipes her face with the back of her hand and, looking exhausted, walks down the steps.

Since her death, Aunty Tanya Day's family fought for the Victorian state public drunkenness law to be abolished, and the law is set to be abolished on Melbourne Cup Day in November 2023.

Constable Zachary Rolfe faced a murder trial for the shooting of Kumanjayi Walker. He was acquitted of all criminal charges by an entirely non-Indigenous jury. It was the first time a Northern Territory police officer was charged with an Aboriginal death in custody since the Royal Commission into Aboriginal Deaths in Custody in 1991. There have been at least 517 Aboriginal deaths in custody since the release of the Commission's report. No Australian police officer has ever been convicted of an Aboriginal death in custody.

9 May, 2018.

This X is the axis along which wages crawl in economic graphs, with productivity and profits soaring upwards together into the corner like a banker's hollow smile. This X means an early death for those who can no longer afford to live in Australia.

Lots of morning coffee is being clutched at the Australian Council of Trade Union's first Change the Rules strike. The sun is bright on Lygon St and the crowd smells of aftershave, perfume, and cigarettes. People hand out socialist newspapers reading "Corporate Greed is Bleeding Australia Dry!" I overhear conversation between guys in hoodies and boots, *They're saying $85 billion in tax cuts.* The union initialisms on every side—NIW AEU NIMF MUA CFMEU—teachers, nurses, midwives, maritime and construction workers and more. The Greens triangle marches around above the crowd on invisible arms. A woman laughs on the way past, *I've got the wrong shoes, the wrong shoes.* I see fierce veteran Boomer activists with grey-streaked hair. The union's Eureka flag in Indigenous colours flicks in the wind among the Australian Services Union (clerical workers). Big white blokes welcome each other with big handshakes. *How are ya, mate? Where you bin workin'?* I hear the growing boom of a helicopter, the first of the day. The socialist red flag flying high atop Trades Hall. An Indigenous man in a knitted beanie wears his nation's flag proudly as a cape. Luke Hilakari, Trades Hall Secretary, tells us that we are 60,000 people strong on the streets of Melbourne. *We do not wanna be a country of the working poor. For so long, big business have been feeding us crumbs, like we're pigeons. We're not pigeons. When the 1% have as much as 70%, the system is broken. Inequality is at a 70-year high. It hasn't been this high since the Great Depression.* Luke booms, *Do you want equal pay for women?* The crowd roars *YES!*

A speaker introduces Mahani, who is here representing 100,000 farm workers with the National Union of Workers. Overwhelmingly casual. No penalty rates. Paid cash-in-hand well below the legal minimum wage. Mahani introduces herself as a migrant farm worker from Malaysia. She has a high woman's voice and a Malaysian accent. She sounds a little shrill through the speakers—who doesn't when they have to pro*ject*?—but her message is clear. *We need work rights! We need better future!* Speaking of undocumented migrant workers' harsh black-market labour conditions, she says, *We need amnesty now!* White blokes who'd roared their support for Luke now stand around scoffing and laughing, wincing at her voice through the speakers. These moments don't make it into the press coverage, but they're some of the most important to remember. I am reminded that solidarity is not a status we achieve, but a horizon we work towards, and that our movements regularly fail people of colour. Mahani, migrant woman of colour, activist and union leader, braves our crowd's bullshit and our country's hostility to stand up to speak for 100,000 farm workers being exploited all over Australia.

A speaker booms, *What does the government think when they think that they can turn around and tell youse who you can elect as union leaders? I say to all of you, people from all unions, when they came after them, they come for all of us!* Sally McManus, Secretary of the Australian Council of Trade Unions, the peak trade union body, tells the crowd that 40% of Australian workers are in insecure work. 732 corporations paid not one cent of tax. 62 people who earned more than $1 million in a year paid not one cent of tax, not even the Medicare levy. Guys giggle about the difficulty of holding signs in the wind. *Nah I'm good holding the flag here, might swap when I need a cigarette. Won't have one yet though, might burn the flag!* A tune starts up from a brassy marching band behind us. I first heard the tune as a kid in country Queensland, knowing it by the earlier folk song lyrics, *John Brown's body lies a-mouldering in the grave* overlaid with the union movement's 1915 lyrics to become their rallying song, "Solidarity Forever." But I still hear *John Brown's body* in the melody, and it only makes the union's version more urgent—the failure of the union is a body in the grave.

The National Tertiary Education Union, my crew, in purple

shirts and whistles. *Education Not Exploitation! Casuals Against Casualisation!* There are lots of young women among us. *Postgrads and casuals on strike! No more unpaid work!* Pink-scarfed, purple-haired, chatty, checking phones. Someone starts up a snare drum. A woman unionist tells us that the stereotype of a unionist is a man with a hard hat, but in Australia but the average unionist is a woman with a degree. Among the union's contingent at a later rally, I hear Nic Kimberly, a casual academic, address the crowd. The Australian Catholic University threatened Nic with revoking his PhD scholarship for criticising casualisation in progressive national newspaper *The Age*. His voice gets stronger and more defiant as he says, *So what did I do to respond? I became the union branch President!* In the crowd, the conversation continues around me. *It's not about someone coming to uni to have that transformative experience anymore. It's about getting bums on seats, and not long while we're making money.* Elsewhere, I hear, *we've got a problem with homeless students.* A silver-haired union woman waves to kids in the windows on Lygon St. The chilly winds of late Autumn blow down Victoria St as we walk through the intersection. Bystanders bop to the brass band as we slowly march. *A first degree shouldn't cost a mortgage!* Onlookers grin, take phone videos. Flyers, flags and protesters have filled the street as far as the eye can see from Swanston to Queen St. A woman of colour wears leopard-print, sunnies and huge heart earrings with *Militant* in curvy script inside. The other side, I later see, reads *Feminist.* A flag flicks across the back of my neck, a surprising intimacy. A red-and-black jester-clothed trumpet player is cheered by the crowd. A sign says *I'm young and insecure and so is my work!* There is a crisp wind from behind and welcome pockets of sunshine and the slow spin of autumn leaves lifted on winds between skyscrapers. Smiling women in office windows wave invisible flags with us in solidarity. Photographers perch on every tram stop and plinth along our way to capture our march's glorious sprawl.

Flyers paper the fancy cars parked in the middle of Bourke St. A kid in blue gumboots and a Superman shirt is wheeled through the march—despite chants, clappers, trumpets, and drums—completely asleep.

We pick up marchers, chants and energy as we make our way down Swanston St. A guy faceplants on the tram island and is helped by everyone. *You right, brother?* A voice reads out a news update behind me, *City streets shut down as 50,000 march.* A grumpy skinny corporate guy in a tight blue suit cuts through the crowd at an intersection. A speaker says, *It's about the young people we work with every day. They are ripped off in their jobs. They're forced to jump through hoops to access inadequate Newstart* (the unemployment welfare payment). *We don't want them to become the working poor of the future.* Troy Carter tells the crowd about the Esso (ExxonMobil) workers: *Sacked, then offered their jobs back at up to 40% less.* It would be 742 days before the strike ended in a deal. Troy speaks about the effect on his family, on his children being bullied at school. *My children have forced themselves into a shell to avoid being rejected. When I stood outside UGL* (the contractor for Esso), *their Payroll Officer yelled, "How's your kids, Troy?" and laughed.* Colin Long speaks, Secretary of the Victorian National Tertiary Education Union: *50% of undergraduate teaching is performed by casuals, many working casually for 5, 10, 15 years. Low super, no leave. It should be a scandal that one of our members found herself unable to leave an abusive relationship because of being totally financially dependent. Our researchers find cures for cancer, we develop renewable energy.* We write to chart the course of the history we are living. *Are you ready to change the rules?* The farm workers' signs, stark and true: NO PICKERS NO FOOD NO FUTURE.

This X means early death for the workers whose wages have flatlined along the X axes of economics graphs. But while the union movement lives there is always hope for a better future.

15 March, 2019.

It's a clear day, sunshine, with a cool breeze outside the Old Treasury Building on Spring St as the crowd gathers for the global School Strike 4 Climate. An old woman with a walker, moving slowly, sunnies and a straw hat, makes her way through the intersection, a sign on her walker saying *1.5 to stay alive, stop climate change!* Indigenous men in white paint clack clapsticks from atop a plinth, gum branches held to their comrades. A teenage girl's voice rises above the crowd. *My name's Gaia, I'm a 17-year-old school striker and I'm here because I want a future on this planet. We acknowledge that we meet on the stolen lands of the Boon Wurrung people and there is no climate justice without First Nations justice.* The men raise their arms from the plinth and roar their strength. Two choppers hover over the intersection. *Striking for our future*, says a sign covered in sparkly writing and kids' drawings. *Stop giving us an excuse to skip school!* The speaker continues, *Make some noise if this is your first protest!* I hear a roar reaching down the hill past Treasury Gardens that warms my heart. Grey-haired activists look on and smile. The sign pun/meme game at this protest is exquisite. My friends see me writing down slogans and make sure that I've noted the choicest quotes: *There was one earlier, a picture of Tony Abbott* (the ultra-conservative former Prime Minister filmed eating a raw onion like an apple)*, said "No onions on a dead planet." Kids wouldn't have to act like politicians if politicians didn't act like kids! Prime Minister has a pet rock—He's so coal.* A handful of girls and a woman appear on the balcony of the Old Treasury building before being shooed off. A young woman's voice across the crowd: *20,000 people are here, 20,000!* and we roar. An Indigenous speaker says: *We need to listen to my Country, to the Law of my ancestors.* A sign says, *I came here because I hate Melbourne weather. Climate change is not an elective!* I hear, *There's a drone!* and I see it, tiny creature hovering smoothly with its black legs. *Grumpy old man who supports students. Don't frack the future* alongside the Midwives' Union. *Teachers for Climate Justice.* A speaker says that 100 companies cause 71% of climate change. An Aboriginal woman is walking with her kids, something written in the elegant rhythms of an Indigenous language over an illustration of the Aboriginal flag and the earth. A translation on the back of the sign says *Little faces, powerful hearts, we stand together.* I ask her, *What language is that?* She replies *Gunnai!* with pride. *It's beautiful.* My queer community are here: *Gay for Renewables!*

We listen to the urgent speeches of teenage girls in the microphone, *Everyone who's an activist and also a student, get everyone at your school*, the crowd cheers, whistles and kazoos trumpet from all around. *Keep the Earth clean, it's not Uranus.* I see the rainbow sheen of fresh-blown bubbles rising from the corner near the Treasury Gardens and floating away. We cluster in the shade of the buildings at the edge of the crowd. A baby in a sling on her mum's front is holding a cardboard sign saying *Nap strike for climate.* Kids are front and centre on the steps of Old Treasury. The crowd is happy, energetic, diverse, loud, and dynamic. *Climate change is union business* on the black shirt of a charismatic fat lady with red lipstick who's walking a little girl by the hand. *Coal: Drop it coz it's HOT*. Marchers have brought a massive rainbow flag, silky and tall as two people. I notice later that it says WE ARE UNION. *Proud teacher! Scared human.* Kids' fresh chalk drawings fade between the tram lines on the street, trees and earth in pinks and greens. Kids in school uniforms sit on the curb, grinning into their milkshakes. *I'd rather be at school than telling you to do your job.* A sign says *My kids are revolting—proud dad*. Tourists and businesspeople and shoppers look on happily from the street. I love the way the kids' use of pop culture fuels their activism. *Every disaster movie starts with scientists being ignored.*

The crowd has poured into Treasury Gardens, and there are dogs barking, picnics, kids cheering, a speaker announcing solidarity with the Standing Rock Sioux water protectors. White women in yellow high-vis security vests, *Where's the baaand, Jenny, I thought you said there was gonna be a band?!* A speaker passionately exclaims, *We are not your enemy! Farming communities are not your enemy! We are the ones being hit worst by climate change*. A woman's voice in the mic: *I'm glad to know I'm not the only one who goes home every night who thinks, what is going to happen to my kids when I'm dead and gone?* A speaker says *My dad is a farmer. His dad is a farmer. I wanted to be a farmer but there won't be anything left to FARM*. The police estimate 50,000 people in Melbourne alone.

Attending the Melbourne protest of Donald Trump's inauguration on 21 January 2017, a friend asks me, *What's the point?* I say, *We have to do something, we have to let them know that this is not okay*. Critiquing the dismissal of activist events as "preaching to the choir," Rebecca Solnit writes:

> [Researcher Erica Chenoweth] concluded that only around 3.5 percent of a population was needed to successfully resist or even topple a regime non-violently. In other words, to create change, you don't need everyone to agree with you; you just need some people to agree so passionately that they will donate, campaign, march, risk arrest or injury, possibly prison or death. Their passionate conviction may influence others. Ideas originate at the margins and migrate inwards to succeed; insisting that your idea must have arrived rather than be traveling is to miss how change works.

This X is the death of all life, what awaits us if we do nothing, if we don't do enough, the X for extinction in the centre of Extinction Rebellion's hourglass logo. But this X also means hope. Our hope lies in the fight not yet over, in the leadership of young people and Elders who show us the way. The hourglass is not finished, but time is running out.

This story begins and ends with the X that means both death and hope.

Three Xs, two strikes, one message: Solidarity forever.

Dr. Ariadne Starling is an award-winning writer from Melbourne working in literary essays, sex writing, and queer literature. Her work explores sexuality, disability, neurodiversity, culture, identity, and social justice. She has won 5 national and international scholarships and 16 awards for academic and creative writing—starting at the age of 11. She was shortlisted for the Overland Fair Australia Essay Prize and the City of Melbourne Lord Mayor's Creative Writing Award for Narrative Nonfiction. She has published in *Transcultural Studies*, *Colloquy*, *Cordite Poetry Review*, and *Verity La*.

"The X That Means Both Death and Life" originally appeared in *Unlikely Stories* in July 2023.

Tisha b'Av

Esther Alter

When Israel finished its retraction of the rights of all immigrants, women, queers, and others, and reduced the Knesset to an advising body for a permanent non-elected executive, when that nation stripped away the rights of the remaining Palestinians, all rights, until they were but animals before the law, the day came when soldiers entered East Jerusalem and rounded up everyone and sent them on trucks to the Negev to live or die, it did not matter, and those who stayed behind were annihilated by missiles, the hospitals, the schools, the people, all gone—on that day, the bulldozers at last arrived on the Temple Mount and drove through the protesters like Moses parting the Red Sea and in the end it was so sudden, one moment there was a shrine, the next debris, and from some of that very material the Israelis began to build the long-yearned-for Third Temple and when it was done, so too ended an entire era of Judaism, and good riddance—it had served us well enough for two thousand years but we turned to the East and saw a Bet-Ha'Mikdash and a Kohen Gadol and a Sanhedrin, and now all halacha was obsolete, no reason to do teshuvah when we now had korbanot, and so we returned, millions of us, though not everyone, not the converts or the half-Jews or the queers or the atheists or the undesirables—and when we arrived we hugged and kissed and danced and ate and sang and drank from the West Bank's aquifer, we drank and drank until not one drop remained, and we cried out, we were stricken with such terrible thirst that our skin cracked and our health failed and many of us died yet still no amount of rain could replenish what we had taken, and then came the floods, all around the world sparing not the Holy Land, submerging Tel Aviv and Haifa and all the lowlands, and then came such a terrible storm that the parched hills couldn't contain it and there were landslides, whole towns were lost, and the sea swelled, and the remainder of us fled to the Temple Mount and under a gray sky huddled and held each other's hands as the water of the deeps lapped at our feet.

July 2023

Esther Alter is a trans Jewish short story writer and game designer. Her fiction has appeared in *Baffling Magazine*, *khōréō*, and the print anthologies *Luminescent Machinations* and *Other Covenants: Alternate Histories of the Jewish People*. Her games can be found at https://subalterngames.itch.io Follow her at @esther_alter@mastodon.social

Wade

Olumide Manuel

The ruins sitting quiet on the belly
of the earth, the slush of water filling
the bleached street, the mouth of deluge
raising a toast to white hills, and
the farmers' agony and its harvest basket
of tears, are the bodies of this poem
sickening my inside like a claw.

My wet body, a flotsam at edge
with the drenched cushions
scattered across the void, through
the roil of heavens, the sepia grief.

How the sky unheld a dirty flood
against a city clogged with neglect,
robust at the throat of its sewerage.

Tell God, this city is not a kitchen basin.
Say His name is near to the homeless teeth
gnashing in the dripping cold. Say i body
enough colours in my protest to rainbow
this wreckage into a fleeing breeze.

Yet every second of feet-sweeping,
I dread if the mouth of flood is shallow
enough to hold my head above the waters,
trembling with step towards a dry exile.

Olumide Manuel, NGP IX, is a writer, a biology teacher and an environmentalist. He has been a nominee for the Pushcart Prize and the winner of Aké Climate Change Poetry Prize 2022. His chapbook, *Hopemonger*, won the Nigerian NewsDirect Chapbook Award 2022. His works have been published on *Magma Poetry*, *Trampset*, *Uncanny Magazine*, *Agbowó Magazine*, *Up the Staircase Quarterly*, *Frontier Poetry*, and elsewhere.

A Chanterelle Empress & Porcini Prince at the Precipice of the World

Chanlee Luu

For K Phung

My best male friend in college was a fun guy.
Vietnamese—we share the same "middle name"—
Le, although his is Lê and mine Lệ. That extra
dot carried a lot of weight. Lê, an unassuming pear.
My dad insisted 丽 meant beautiful.

My aunt insisted Lì meant crying.
Names get complicated when navigating
three worlds. Consider the mushroom,
not flora, not fauna, but a secret
third thing. A bounty hiding in plain sight—

like the two of us. Our majesty masked
by expectations of Asian America.
He "wanted" to become a doctor,
a pediatrician trading lollipops
and smiles to snotty kids.
I chose to be a chemical engineer,
a magician converting matter
to fuel like fungi—

our wholeness deep underground,
right next to our group of visible
queer friends. I wonder if he ever
considered death, a self-destruction
on the way to reincarnation.

But he was too practical

and artful to consider such
a dismal reinvention.

He worried about my future.
Told me to get a credit card,
walked me home, afraid
I'd be taken in the dark.
In my head, that was the moment

we became potential beard and wig—
a mess of manicured hair
to be presented to parents,
if needed. As if our mothers' imaginations
were limited by the pebbled paths of their pasts.
As if a spouse is a requirement
for attainment of the American Dream.

But deep in the woods, nấm
show us the way to immortality—
how to pen our poison,
how to draw the world
in networks of beauty,
and how to be
a truffle in the rough.

My favorite picture of us is after
we won *Risk: Global Domination*,
my stupid croakies hanging
from my neck like enokis
and his hair shiny and black
like the inside of a glazed portobello.

Both of us in lime green,
mid-laughter, knowing we have all
the time in the world.

Chanlee Luu is a Vietnamese-Chinese American writer. She received her MFA in creative writing from Hollins University, and BS in chemical engineering from UVA, where she competed in poetry slams. She writes about identity, pop culture, science, politics, and everything in between. She can be found on Twitter @ChanleeLuu, and her work in *Snowflake Magazine*, *the gamut mag*, *Cutbow Quarterly*, *Tint Journal*, *Honey Lit*, *The Offing*, and *diaCRITICS*, among others.

Riis Beach

Dina Abdulhadi

Aureliano Segundo ask[ed the Arabs] with his usual informality what mysterious resources they had relied upon so as not to have gone awash in the storm... one after the other, from door to door, they returned a crafty smile and a dreamy look, and without any previous consultation they all gave the answer:
"Swimming."

—*Gabriel Garcia Marques,* One Hundred Years of Solitude

Leave home. Take what
I want to survive.
The rest: waterlogged,
pawned, landfilled
by landlords, emptied
photographs of Petra,
Pyramids, child eyes
kneaded into layers of
pecan shells, diapers,
coke cans, chicken bones.
Chew pith, sweet with bitter.
Know father could carry
less over the Jordan River
and all waters after that.
How he loved even
the worst fried chicken.

I only wear 20%
of the identities I own
80% of the time. Remember
sunk costs of saving
those who don't want my help.
Good daughter, ungrateful
American, robot. Learn
organic chemistry and become

the Teflon they say I am.
Give one past me away,
everyday. Declutter sorrys,
hoarded words, lab coat,
hair straightener, southern drawl.
Fill a bag with memory
clutter. Use a different bag
to control my breathing.

Take pictures from
river to unattainable sea,
of any journey to the ocean
for when I forget what
I promised myself, and him.
Replace memories evicted,
displace inheritance of displacement,
so I could savor the shore
while I was still young.
One more reminder: a wound,
a hope, a desire expands
to fill the space I allow it.

The River Jordan dries up
by baptism held at a rifle's end
while the rising Western seafront
advances on its deathwish.

My promise: I breathe life and
don't release a thing to the sea.
It is filled with enough trash
human intention already,
hoards everything we give it.

Take with you only
what you want to survive.
Trust the small creatures
who tread these waves of passage,
coiling your hair to currents,
kissing your salty skin.

Dina Abdulhadi is a Palestinian American writer and ex-scientist from the US South. A 2021 Brooklyn Poets Fellow, her writing has appeared in *Mizna*, *The Worcester Review*, and *Breakwater Review*. She is based in Brooklyn, NY. References in her work to the ongoing genocide and mass displacement of the Palestinian people are not metaphorical, and this genocide is not inevitable. She asks that whatever grief this poem stirs in you moves you to action to resist this genocide.

Climate injustice

Lovely Raju

1
(The Cyclone)

An owl cries for her baby.
Dead body is found nowhere.
The storm again is a good
Killer of unborn dreams.

My father mourns for the tree.
The trunk lies on the ground,
Sleeps and soon will die.

He planted it years ago.

2
(The Wildfire)

Heaven now turns hell.
Wildfire burns the feathers
Of the parrot, now she crawls,
Crawls to breathe a little more,

Fire growls behind the tail.
Death waves before fatigued eyes,
Yet she hopes to live again.

3
(The Drought)

Sun is trying to burn
The scalps of my parents
In the paddy land.

They wonder if the sweat
Acted like the water.

A little white cloud turns
Into a canopy over their
Shoulders, but mother wants it
To be fierce and to pour in the land as rain.

4
(The Poverty)

Salt water strangles the crops,
Makes us starve and my
Old granny will die
Soon of hunger.

Climate Crisis in My (Un)known Dream

Lovely Raju

(1)

A giant human shadow on earth
Engulfs the ocean and cloud
Remains arid now heavy hearted
Angel there praying for light.

Mother sitting in the sun.
In the kitchen she cooks something
She stands still, tap is on
Basin is clogged, water soon
Floods our planet.

Star dust around her face,
My son playing in the backyard
Fears the shadow, I say
It is your granny, look.

Mother comes down now sits
In the air right beside my boy.
In the kitchen she moves and
Cries, no sound, I see her chop
A big onion, and no one is there
Outside my son and mother.

(2)

A coffin
We were only two
The main door was closed.

Indoor that goes to other room
Stood alone,
No path, before us, a wall
We saw everything through.

The earth was shaking now from inside
Soon maybe, soon wave would explode,

The disaster, the homeless people
Wandering under the sky

The earth looked dull,
The climate was so indomitable.

Someone said, stay, you are safe there.

Lovely Raju is originally from Bangladesh. He holds a BS in Applied Chemistry and Chemical Engineering from the University of Rajshahi. Seeking to nurture his poetic talents further, he pursued an MFA in creative writing from the University of Notre Dame. Raju has worked as an assistant editor at Action Books, an international press for poetry and translations. His interests include ecopoetry, social justice poetry, and dream poetry. His debut full-length poetry book, *HOPE,* is out now from the Finishing Line Press. His second full-length poetry collection, *Inside Violence Violence Inside,* is forthcoming from FlowerSong Press. You can find him on Instagram @poetry_poem_cares

Civil Disobedients

Joanna Streetly

It's one in the morning & my daughter is missing
          I lie in the dark car, a crate of tools by my head
(I should be calling her father)

We started out together, peaceful citizens walking the logging road, shaded
      by old growth trees, police helicopters, yellow-taped exclusion zones
that moved in puppet-string tugs—government toying with prey.

We carried contraband: for me, innocuous diapers, sunscreen, water
        sundries needed by arrestees; for her, makings of hard locks
crow bars, zeal, reasons why, bags of cement, sixty pounds & sixteen years

of life slung on her back, (I should be combing the road for her,
          the passing terror of search lights, boots vanishing into bush
as night-ops quads roar by . . .)

***

It all went wrong at the checkpoint
          shouts in the dusk, AAAAAs of arm-folded, spread-legged men
bowling pins in an alley of smug trucks, exhaling idle patience

exhaust blending with sudden dense fog, the droplets
          golden in blinding headlights. I was a distractor, supposed
to take my riteful passage, while the concrete crew detoured

a deer trail, eight men, one girl, (mine—missing—she is sixteen
          & I am her imperfect mother,) but fresh rules had been concocted
the platoon of cops, fingers twitching, no point in a night fight

& she had already become the dark forest
          no phones, no radios, no way to say *come back*
tho' my silent mouth did its best, over & over

& now I do as I'm told, lie in the dark car
        a crate of tools by my head, think everything
mothers think when children are missing, in fog

in darkness, on strange mountains, with strange men, (I should
        have arms enough to reach her, enough to wrap the forest
not let go, I should—*I don't even know their names!*)

* * *

Is it enough that we all believe in trees? That this logging
        of ancients has broken us—will break the sky?
Two am footsteps, my daughter breathless

the chase, the hiding, the nearly-being-caught, the stashing of goods
      no map of where, the newly-minted friends *Foxglove, Felix, Peace,*
my daughter, here, unlost, unhurt, un-scarred, un-scared.

We feign sleep in a theatre of gravel, windsung by ghosts
      of once-were-trees. At dawn we crowd the barrier, breast the yellow tape
move to higher ground, where—cat & mouse—there is more tape

fresh & festive, a thin blue line of uniforms, weapons ready
        while we have only songs & selves, limp bodies
& though we defer logging, ride a paddy wagon, still the trees we came for
fall
& fall.

Joanna Streetly is the published author of five books. Her work can also be found in in *Best Canadian Poetry 2024* and *Best Canadian Essays 2017,* as well as many anthologies and literary magazines. She recently won the *Cirque* poetry contest and has been short-listed for the VanIsle Collective Prize, the FBCW Literary Writes Poetry Contest and the *The Spectator's* Shiva Naipaul award for outstanding travel writing. In 2015 she was long listed for the Canada Writes Creative Non-fiction Prize. She is passionate about trees, oceans, birds—nature in general—and has lived in the unceded territory of the Tla-o-qui-aht for over thirty years in a floathouse she built herself. In 2018-2020, she was the inaugural Tofino Poet Laureate.

Photo credit Jen Steele

Pearls of Wisdom

Kirsty Greenwood

Kirsty is an illustrator who works mainly within the realm of short fiction stories both for print and online publications. With experience in many aspects of artwork and the advantage of an illustrative mind-set, her passion is for imagery that accompanies literature based in the surreal, the Gothic and folk tales; she has also exhibited her works internationally, and more recently, 'Metamorphosis', the fabric she designed for and in collaboration with The Monkey Puzzle Tree art fabrics and wallcoverings, was winner of 'Best in British Product Design' at the Hotel Designs Brit List Awards 2021. Motivated by pareidolia, ephemeral visual misunderstanding, ocular strangeness, nightmares, dreams and fleeting glimpses of unreality; inspired by Faerie tales, folklore, myths and legends, transformation, aboriginal cultures and Quixotism, Kirsty works in traditional mediums such as paint, pencils and inks on home-made marbled papers.With her work focused on the idea of embracing change, she uses mark-making methods such as marbling to create a base for her images and then uses the traditional techniques of drawing, inking and paint washes to further make the scene, picking out details to promote the telling of tales through images filled with narrative, allure, and creatures from around the allegorical world.

50% off Venus Fly Traps

Kelsey Day

pretty thing come closer
your jaw so tense in the gardening aisle
I brush my knuckles against the
trigger hairs on your mouth, ask about your
waterwheel & sundew cousins,
when you last digested an arachnid, I
admire your hunger, the biology of it,
I read that it takes a tenth of a second
for your teeth to snap
down but you don't close your
lips around my thumb when I touch you
you like a certain kind of prey
don't you
but you know your kind are
declining in the wilderness
not enough acid in the soil
we preserve you in the aisles like this one
we keep you alive
get in the cart
show me you're grateful
show me how you want this
don't you want something to eat
won't you
open wide for me

Kelsey Day is a queer poet from southern Appalachia. Their work can be found in *Freeman's, The Appalachian Review, Washington Square Review, The Foundationalist, Brave Voices*, and *Our Shared Memory Collective*, and has been nominated for the Pushcart Prize, the Penrose Poetry Prize, and Best of the Net.

Fear of Pipes and Shallow Water

William O. Balmer

beside the crick a few cm deep
it glides across spilt jumbles of rock
curling trails of unctuous vapor
spin fractals up my arm from a stub
pinched between fingers white smoke
fades away into the glare off the water

the crick chatters
the din of each flow a voice
a dinner party. the audience hushes
itself after the orchestra has finished tuning
and for a moment i am with them all
waiting in anticipation

if i were a writer
id described the way i slurped
from the elementary school water fountain
as greedy. it wasn't greed that tapped politely on shoulders
just lust for the cool clear taste of water
dribbling down my shirt
soaking my collar

before they installed
the burnished steel features
with stop motion sensors to fill
reusable bottles the fountain was
porcelain and the pressure so low i would
place my lips against rusting metal to slurp
until one day the porcelain cracked and
covered the vinyl tile in a thin sheet
of invisible water

when i grew taller
the world got wider
i had to kneel at the
altar but at least they fixed
the pressure so that the water flowed
freely into my mouth

basement
old building with
a gas stove but no hood
and half the ceiling covered in those
false ceiling tiles they had in school covering
dusty pipes in my first apartment

pipes from the highrise condos
drain a few miles up from where
i tempt the water with my dangling feet
watching the heron pick at an old doritos bag
there's a sign up by the dog park
that gleams with whatever magic
makes hazard vests reflective
and warns the reasonable not to
drink or swim or wade
but an elderly couple pass
carrying their sneakers
ankle deep in sparkling water

not even the fancy
chrome fountains
survived the purge
and we laughed in
high school when one
day we came in to see
each and every fountain
wrapped in plastic bags
and they told us the pipes
were full of lead and had
been for years and we heard
from friends the school over

one sink had 58,000 ppb
and i imagined the tens
of thousands of us could
all be friends now that we
had superpowers

and i remember kissing the faucet
and kneeling in prayer to greedily
slurp and trying to slide down
the soaked hallway on paper towels
but i never noticed the smoke stack
next to the school like the cigarette in my hand whispering
tendrils of gray into sparkling translucence they
said laced the soil with heavy metals
and i can't warn the deer off the
crick without scaring her
but i wish she knew

pipes yearn to spill and i thought i knew why
someone might bleed too keep them from their veins
but when i heard water splashing in the living room
and desperately stuffed my clueless cat in the carrier and
sloshed through the ankle deep water to pull my most
valuable whatever out of the basement i felt some
tiny part of why folks bleed

kids my age made memes of
the old commercials for the class action
and mesothelioma was always accompanied by laughter
and ive never worked a mine so when the water stopped running
i was throwing out the soggy broken false ceiling tiles with my couch
when i realized the reason the water looked so nasty brackish
draining down the walls filling my living room was
cause the wrapping on the pipes that
were hidden by the tile were
fireproof

pipes in my heart
strain with the fear
of every particle
inside me but
everyday i
take another piece
of this broken world
into myself forever and
inhale and when the heron
is finished with the doritos bag
my fear of pipes and shallow water
will link me to billions like me and maybe
i won't be a kid when they split the next hill
to run a pipe and ill join you on the line hand in hand
and we can use these superpowers we've all been given to plug
leaks and clean spills so that when i take my place in the heavenly host
every particle of plastic embedded within me
will shimmer like the surface of this crick.

William Otto Balmer spends their days (or, nights?) as an astronomer at the Johns Hopkins University, where they take pictures of planets in other solar systems. At night (or, during the day?) they write speculative fiction and poetry. *Fear of Pipes and Shallow Water* is their first published poem. They can be found online at www.astrowill.page. They live in Baltimore, Maryland with their cat Morgoth.

The Battle for Florida

David Holloway

I moved to Florida from Wisconsin when I was ten, but Curtis "Wild Hair" Kensington had been born there. I remember him running across the vacant lots, shirtless with his chaotic hair flying, his skin red from the sun in those pre-sunscreen days. His feet were so tough from going barefoot that the sandspurs that pained the rest of us bounced from the callused soles of his Floridized feet.

We grew up as neighbors in a Florida suburb built over a bulldozed orange grove. The grove itself had been planted over a razed thicket of sandspurs and slash pine. Possums, frogs, the occasional alligator, and snakes never got the suburb memo. Whenever it rained, wild creatures showed up on porches and in garages.

These included the impressive eastern diamondback I found in my garage. Hissing at one end and buzzing at the other, thick as a bicycle tire, it turned to look at me with an air of boredom. As if to say, "I was here long before you and I'll be here long after you've gone."

By the time I found a shovel to kill it, the snake had disappeared. That snake or his cousins would show up in driveways, swimming pools, and manicured lawns throughout my years in Florida, reminding me who really owned the place.

When we were in sixth grade, we joined the junior sailing club and splashed around the bay in little sailing dinghies. They called the tiny boats Optimist Prams. Once when I was a hundred yards from everyone else, an enormous creature, longer than my boat, swam up next to me. He rolled on his side to look me in the eye and showed me his sharp white teeth. People gush over the dolphin's cute smile, but I recognized it as a warning, not a welcome.

Senior year all of us on the football team gathered magic mushrooms from a local cow pasture and ate them after losing the last game. We passed out in Matheson Hammock Park and woke in a single huge cocoon of chigger-infested Spanish moss. We crawled out covered in red swollen chigger bites, itching, and moaning. Curtis blamed a vividly remembered alien abduction.

The state decided to expand our little town's perfect beach by dredging up rough coral stones from the bottom of the gulf and throwing them onto the smooth sugar sand, trying for more of a good thing. They ran out of funds before covering the acres of sharp, rough stones with sand, and the prized beach resembled a blasted moonscape for decades.

Curtis loved weird Florida and took me to visit Spook Hill in Lake Wales to watch my car roll uphill. He took the ghost tour at the Riddle House in Palm Beach and swore that he once saw the elusive Florida Skunk-Ape, the state's favorite cryptid.

Curtis attended Seances in Cassadaga, home to more active spiritualists per capita than anywhere else on earth. His favorite medium, Nika, had moved to Florida from Dubrovnik as a child. Nika had a spirit guide named Tiger Miccosukee, a Seminole Indian in life. At the last séance Curtis attended, Nika asked Tiger about the future of Florida. The spirit's sobs were deafening.

By the time I went to college in South Carolina, high tides had begun to cover the sidewalks, lawns, and roads in my little Florida town. During one visit home, Curtis drove my car through a puddle that turned out to be a deep-flowing stream. It pushed my old Honda Civic off the road and into a canal. Curtis waded out laughing, drunk with relief at his escape. His joy washed away my anger as quickly as the flood had swept my car away.

Curtis called me to say that the beefalo herd escaped their ranch in Ft. Lauderdale again, causing havoc by wandering out onto I-95. He said that they were the perfect livestock for Florida. Ridiculously tough and too dumb to understand fences.

I got a job in Charlotte, North Carolina, and my friend stayed in Florida. The last time I talked to him, he described his house. "Right on the mouth of the river. I can smell the stink of low tide from the screened porch." Three weeks later, Hurricane William roared through with a thirty-foot storm surge, washing Curtis and his house away. They never found his body.

I visited for my 25th high school reunion. I drove out to the beach for old times' sake, planning to drink rum and enjoy the psychedelic sunset. Florida gives great sky. I hadn't heard about the latest red tide. The stench hit me like a pro linebacker. Hundreds of dead fish of all types and sizes, along with the bloated body of a huge dead manatee, rocked back and forth in the gentle surf. Even the gulls wouldn't scavenge their too-noxious flesh. Florida had signed a suicide pact.

I keep a football-sized horse conch shell that I found on Clearwater Beach on the coffee table in my living room. Visitors insist on holding it up to the side of their heads and listening for the sound of the ocean. When I listen, I hear Florida whispering, calling, cursing. I don't hear the hiss of waves, but a fat snake's belly scraping along the concrete floor of my garage.

David Holloway writes from Savannah, Georgia. He has lived most of his life in the South, primarily Florida, and has always loved spending time in nature and reading about others' experiences in the natural world. His publications include stories published in *Abandon Journal, The Mad River Review, The Offbeat, Agnes and True*, and *Gargoyle*, among other magazines. Due to early traumatic experiences, he does his best to avoid bagpipes and parrots.

Data, Land, Scape

Koby Omansky

i. Data

Omitted from calculations, all manner of plausible certainty,
this rock of burden bleeding the way oxen do when driven home. Here,
a projection of growth, exponential: a hot bird touches a hot stone. Now,
a graph:
a hot bird touches a hot stone in a hot palm. Next slide: a hot bird touches
a hot stone
in the hot palm of a prophet of profit (*good one, Dan!*) orange horizon
of hot meaning touches a hot bird touches a hot stone, scaled to market
—blood on the wheel and dusk, now. Away to their model homes and
sliding doors that lock.
The charts say what they say, *It's in the bag.*
The men leave the room; the desk chairs spinning like slow planets, *You
killed it in there, man.*

ii. Land

Some places the water comes spitting out the faucet clear as brown.
The rivers are dead; bloat and murk. Brooks that once babbled all day lay
silent under blankets of algae. The men around are dark from roofing
in spring. One leans against a wall
opening a clay brick in his hands. Another points to the busy
writhing in the black socket of a cow and says, *Look—a
dead ringer for somethin alive.* A third reaches for the ground
without thinking,
overcome by a sudden memory of something called a dandelion that sent
wishes into the land.

iii. Scape

But this radioactive swamp was my father's, and his father's father's. Our hurting mud is all God's,
Do not throw my clothes out into the yard of space—where other rock can I go
that doesn't groan under the weight of such need unbearable? Where snow does what snow does
and there is no gold to find at the end of an oil slick rainbow.
Show me a porch that doesn't look out on a circle of grief, show me an Earth
whose people bathe her skin in rivers, and wrap her body in long grass.
Show me the room where the decision was made and the papers drawn up; show me a child
who isn't dead in the alley behind it, eyes cloudy with the first dream ever dreamt
the same dream that awoke the first man to the sputtering embers of the first night,
the same dream that unsettled him with a hope he couldn't name as he looked to the many stars.

Koby L. Omansky is a queer poet and writer focused on the intersections of advocacy, nature, and memory. Her work has appeared in places like *Full Stop Quarterly*, *Sourced Magazine*, *FIVE:2:ONE*, anthologies by Platypus Press and Thoughtcrime Press, and more. She lives and works in Brooklyn.

In the Year 2067 I Will Be 95 Years Old

Sage Tyrtle

1.

The year 2067 is an endless Water War. I am standing in front of what used to be a Pizza Pizza on the corner of Queen and Bathurst, fighting alongside my family, because of course my family is there. I am toothless and my partner's glasses are so scratched they're almost useless and our son has made us armour from old license plates. I am defending my ancient sloshing Aquafina water bottle, blocking a knife thrust with M3F 949 MISSOURI.

2.

The year 2067 is finding the raspberries the deer missed. The deer, who make such harrumphs when startled I have named them Aunt Hortense, Aunt Bertha, Nosy Gladys. I cut the raspberries in half to make them last longer and they are somehow better than the brown sugar pavlova I can still remember eating in an actual restaurant with spotless tablecloths. Walls. A ceiling. But mostly human beings. Human beings inhabiting their warm and glorious skin, breathing, walking, words spilling with such careless ease out of their mouths, and I didn't know then to catch them. To keep them safe.

3.

The year 2067 is underwater. Everyone is a pirate but no one is very good at it.

4.

The year 2067 is when Dorinda Clifton is crowned Tesla Reincarnate of the Celestial Followers of the Lightbulb and on October 5th when New Jersey does not light up light up like thousands upon thousands of stars but instead remains a stubborn pit of darkness where wolves roam without fear, Dorinda is suffocated in mud, quartered, and—it's rumoured—eaten.

5.

The year 2067 is other people. I've been gone a long time.

6.

The year 2067 is made of concrete and everywhere I look there are brutalist buildings where brutalist authorities are brutal and the too-hot rain never stops and I am scrabbling in the gray gutters with the people I love to find enough coins for a two-hour shelter pod and we are all keeping our heads down, down.

7.

The year 2067 is the year the government is definitely going to do something about climate change.

8.

The year 2067 is dreaming of trees, of oak, of spruce, of hickory. Of the rustle leaves make in a storm. Wandering a chimeric forest of beech, of maple, of chestnut, of bumpy bark as I trail my fingers along the trunk and listen to the sparrows sing to the sky. Of kneeling to watch saplings learning the wonders of sunlight and how to drink the rain. And waking, weeping, to the ceaseless sound of wind moving sand. Whish. Wish. Whish.

9.

The year 2067 is the Dorchester Library. I lead murmuring patrons by candlelight into the open centre and urge them to look up to see the five floors lined with glorious walls of words. The computers, useless now, have been carried away and gutted, turned into goldfish bowls and cat beds. I am dressed in layers and layers of wool to guard against the always-cold and at lunch I go outside. In the weak sunlight the park is covered with readers. Wandering through places that don't exist anymore, telling each other the stories of how to repair. To mend. To leave, this time, nothing but footprints.

Sage Tyrtle's work is available or upcoming in *New Delta Review*, *The Offing*, and *Apex* among others. She's told stories on stages all over the world and her words have been featured on NPR, CBC, and PBS. She runs a low cost online writing workshop collective. Twitter: @sagetyrtle

Still Life

James Cato

The landlord held out a gun. Shara took it from him. She was doing the mother shtick, which meant playing the protector. The landlord didn't know she was only six years older than me. He might rescind his offer if he knew I was a homeless orphan.

Next he presented us with an axe. "The rifle is for rats," he said. He'd spray-tanned his face, drawing a yellow line under his chin. "Hatchet is for the roof. Wait till the water reaches the attic steps, then chop a hole in the ceiling and climb out. I'll pick you up in the boat."

It made sense well enough. The house standing behind us was free, so long as we kept watch over it. If kids came around and arsoned the place, it could torpedo the flooding insurance. The ocean was filling homes with seawater, and tycoons like the landlord needed their payouts.

"You have striking eyes," he told Shara. His own eyes were hidden behind rainbow sunglasses so I wasn't sure where he was staring. "I always know who I can trust. You have an intensity I like. You'd look good on camera."

She gave him a long slow smile without showing her teeth. It dawned on me that the landlord wanted to sleep with her and that was why he was giving us this chance. He cocked his head at me, maybe reckoning I was not really her son. Hopefuls on the dunes prayed we'd fumble this and leave the house open for looting.

"The house is like a grave in a sense," he said, still tilted. "It's a monument, watching people come and go. The place brings out your inner child. Something about a beach house."

I took in the grass growing from the gutters, the sideskew shutters, the sea teething on the driveway. The yard was marked by stakes and clothesline, and beyond that, railroad tracks arced into the waves, cutting through the wetlands like a ribbon. I never knew what to say to people like the landlord, so I kept quiet.

"We'll take the key, please," Shara said. The landlord dropped a chain into her palm. There were four streaks of makeup on his cheeks covering up something from way back in the day. It looked to me like fingernail scars.

"I'll check on you," he said. "Tally your days. Helps with paperwork."

||||

Four days we scavenged. I dug up a throw rug. The waves delivered glass jars to our front stoop. Shara took a glossy framed painting from the swamp, a still life wrapped in foam. I tallied our days by cutting notches around the frame. Thinking back, these things did seem to appear as if curated for us, but I didn't think it suspicious at the time.

The still life was of a kitchen table with a ceramic jug, a wine glass half-filled, and an assortment of fruit. The most remarkable feature was the faces painted into the fruit—teeth dug into the skins of apples, winking eyes in the pears, miniature scowls in every grape on the vine. It gave the sense of children lurking out of sight, giggling at their dinner table vandalism.

We hung it in the foyer. The house itself had beautiful wood fixtures, ornate paneling, and stone masonry. The walls had been deveined of wires for copper scrap. Shara found the attic by pulling a hinged hatch in her bedroom so a ladder swung down.

I didn't know Shara well. She was superstitious. "Vultures and rats take to a cow before the wolves have even finished nowadays," she said to me once. Strange sounds carried from her room at night and her fingers drew symbols in sand whenever she sat.

She'd adopted me in Cleveland. The city was littered with the skeletons of titan factories. One such factory was full of us orphaned hopefuls, where I spent most of my days on a cot gazing into the swooping beams where I might see a bat. Nobody wanted an adult to adopt us. We knew what they did to children.

But when Shara asked the social workers to line up teenagers for interviews, I volunteered. And when she asked, I told her. My parents had force-fed me nails and glass baked into bread and left me in a basket by the lake when I was a toddler. Thankfully, I passed the sharps without incident and fell asleep. The workers joked I looked like Baby Moses.

Maybe that was why she chose me. Maybe she wanted a companion to run off the men we heard sniffing by our tents like bears. For her part, she provided me a blanket, never tried to mercy-kill me, and we never went hungry. So I didn't comment when she buried things—coins, a wolf claw, a bronze keychain of the Eiffel—calling them symbols of dead power.

The ocean would cover the Earth. Everyone agreed on that. Millions had migrated to the grasslands, springing metropolises overnight, but not Shara. She brought me to the sea to "*ride the wheel of power.*" Knowing what adults did to keep us children safe from this cruel, cruel world, her words stood my hairs on end.

卌 ||||

In the hours leading up to our first storm, the ocean receded and boys and girls ran out over the new territory. They climbed sunken chimneys of the landlord's "Atlantis homes." A dozen rich surfer children called Shara and I *tourists*, sneering. They all lived with their robber baron parents in a shared mansion.

The more modest neighbors, keeping the landlord's other houses, welcomed us. "You're one of us brackish now," they said. "Give a shout." But the nearest of their dwellings were farther away than a scream, huddled across the railroad. None had lived indoors before the landlord's offer, and all worshiped him for his charity. One family even sculpted his bust in their yard from swamp clay.

The rich children did not mix with the brackish kids. I passed three of them as they circled an eel trapped in a tide pool, poking it with sticks till it was dead. Shara had asked me to find fish for dinner, as we had nothing left but beans. On the tide's fringes, dying sardines floated in masses looking like steel wool. The ocean had given Shara exactly what she asked for. I filled two buckets and trotted them home.

The landlord visited our porch as we readied for storm's landing. "I brought wine. Why not talk politics? Have you heard the military abandoned its navy at sea? Let's drink till our teeth turn red!" We did not let him in. There was too much to do. We placed foam noodles in every room. We rolled our carpets and chucked them upstairs.

But he didn't leave. Wherever Shara moved, the landlord's eyes followed, as if he could see straight through the stone. She gestured for me to hand her a chair. "What does he want?" I whispered, peering over the sill as he tracked Shara down the steps.

"Your most terrible fear is inadequate," she said. She tucked hair behind her ear, pausing, and his head snapped still. "When old powers fall, new powers rise to take their place, like crabs moving into empty shells. His power has come from crushing others, and for decades he has thrived. But the wheel no longer rolls his way."

I nodded, watching the silver army of raindrops marching over the sea toward us. I never knew what to make of Shara's words. She pulled the chair down the stairs, *bam-bam-bam*. Then she wedged it under the doorknob as the landlord gazed at her.

"I will tell a story," he called out. "There are three things coming with the ocean. The first is a man who stole power from the gods. By the time they caught him, he'd nabbed their talents of oppression, violence, and eternal life. To punish him, the gods lit his skin with endless fire, melting it to ribbons.

"But the man was no fool. He dove into the sea, where the water quenched the flames quick as they could catch—turning the ocean to his prison. Now, he wanders the floor with the fishes, unable to leave except to die. His ruined skin billows out behind him as he walks alone, waiting for the water to rise—"

The first waves rushed up the driveway. A key slid into the front door's socket.

"It's *MINE*!" cried the landlord. "I'll come in if I want!"

The bolt turned. There was silence, then splashing. We waited, curled into contours of shadows, but no other sound or movement came from the door. In the morning, beside the landlord's prints, tar-black tracks small as bird feet escorted his retreat.

卌 卌 I

Buoys had caught in the porch banisters, and we left them there. The storm was no worse than expected, but it did turn our basement to a lagoon. Lizards hugged the cellar walls, but in the water below crabs thrived. Shara speared them patiently while I shot rats out the window, hoping to reduce our pest load.

Today I scored bigger game. A woodchuck sniffed railroad spikes, unaware of my profile in the window. I lined the notch on the barrel up to its throat. When I fired, the rodent ran, leaping in a great show toward a pile of car parts. I fired again, and it began running awkwardly, twisted. After the third pop, it relaxed with complaining shudders.

"Got one?" Shara asked, startling me. She leaned into my bedroom with a green crab, holding it by the shell. There were always little things about her I didn't understand. Today she wore long brown socks and had managed to keep them dry in the basement, as if the crab had given itself to her.

"Three rats and a woodchuck."

She nodded, letting the claw pinch her thumb. "Anything else?"

"No, but the landlord placed traps in our yard. Big steel-jaw traps." I rubbed the little gun, a new nervous tic. "I don't know why."

"I think I know. During the storm, I saw . . . *friends* in the swamp. They resembled children but were not. They walked on their hands. The wheel is turning fast; we must make peace with trodden things. All those who have wielded power will be ground beneath the wheel. Nail the dead rats around the perimeter, kill no more, and bury anything with power you find."

This is how I found myself hammering dead rats to trees around our property. You could pinch the limp things by the nape like you would a kitten and drive the nail through their hides. I collected tins of shark teeth, jawbones and plastic—all met by Shara's approving nod—to bury. It seemed gifts simply tumbled out of the tide for Shara.

Others had worse luck. MISSING signs fluttered on telephone poles. The group of wealthy children had gone surfing during the storm and vanished. I'd seen so many children euthanized by poor parents that the disappearance of trust-fund brats felt closer to justice than tragedy.

"Hurricane coming," came a voice from the swamp. I turned, clutching my final rat to nail around the property. The landlord clambered through cattails with a tote bag. "Your second storm is always easier than your first. You know, if your mother hoped to frighten looters, you could have asked for something bigger than a rat gun. I've got traps rated for bears."

I shrugged, easing toward the porch, squeezing the hank of hair in my hand in case I needed to throw it at him. The landlord's face rotated away from mine, pointing at Shara through the stones. We had taken planks of driftwood and nailed them rudely over the windows. "I had a son before," the landlord said. "Not like you. A real son. You're more like insurance."

His wide mouth trembled. Without sunglasses, his eyes glittered like little mouths—cataracts were growing up in stalagmite shapes. "When the ocean rises, we'll grow close. I'll rescue you from the roof. There are things coming. I told you about the burning man. How about this: a lobster, caught in a trap on the seafloor. Nutrients drift by. The lobster grows, a huddled, huge thing, alone. Nothing can reach it."

His arm rose suddenly, ripping something putrid from his bag. My woodchuck dangled by a leg—rather, *some* of my woodchuck. Its head and shoulders had been sliced away cleanly as a paper doll. But the carving didn't end there. Empty tendrils in the shape of humanlike legs continued into the torso, as if a tiny man had been whittled from the carcass. "What is *this*?" the landlord hissed. I dropped the rat and fled.

卌 卌 卌

The hurricane raised the water to ground level. Outside, a gale howled, but inside, Shara and I were snug. We took mugs of steam to the cellar steps and watched the lagoon rise. By nighttime, lobsters rippled across the kitchen.

"We envelop ourselves with trodden things like armor," Shara said. "We invite them into our home. Leave some beans out for the rats in the kitchen." She leaned so close to my face that our noses touched.

The landlord pulled at our barriers, asking sweetly for Shara to let him in. "A little company while I dry?" he chanted. "C'mon, sweetheart. I'd like to inspect the damage."

We looked to the door. An arm slithered through a gap in the pallet we'd hammered over a window, fishing for purchase. His eye locked on us through a slit as we edged upstairs.

"The third thing coming with the ocean is a boxcar," he said.

His voice took on an ecumenical lilt, as if he were preaching through the hole. "Coming soon now. Very soon. It was pushed into the sea. Nobody knew what was inside, but they stayed well away."

Through the window, I watched the tide undermine the robber baron mansion on the cliff and carry it off. It sailed into the bay as if nudged by a million fish. The landlord's eyes rose with Shara's legs, step by step. Originally, I had thought this X-Ray vision was a power of his, but understood it now as a power of hers. She made his danger predictable.

This time, when he ran, I heard the patter of feet behind him. Out the attic porthole, a figure no taller than a toddler turned to catch my eye in the grass, falling behind others of its build. It was a patchwork of things, dismembered silhouettes making a little man. Boneless legs ended in blackened meat where belly had been cut into the shape of limbs. When I saw the black grin of the woodchuck I shrunk away.

卌 卌 卌 卌 III

"The landlord is in danger," I said.

Shara's towel-wrapped body twisted to face me. Most people would shout after being surprised straight out of the shower these days, but she merely nodded.

I pressed on. "Something—many somethings—chased him. One of them was wearing the face of the woodchuck."

Shara glanced at me then looked away as if she'd stumbled upon something private. "Why do you think people murder their own children?" she asked at last. "If this world is too awful for the young, why not for their parents?"

I wasn't sure. "People say parents love their children more than themselves."

Shara's eyes softened as she wrung out her hair. Her towel dropped and she strolled over to the wardrobe filled with all the clothes that had swirled into our home for her. "No, that is not why. Parents mercy-kill their children because *their* inner child was killed in a far more terrible way. Children are the most trodden things of all."

I averted my eyes as she approached nude. "So what I saw

you would call children," I said. "Spirits of children. Friends of ours because we've fed rats in the kitchen and stopped eating meat. Is this why you've kept me around? A trodden son to use for armor?"

She touched my chin and kissed me then. "You are not my son. But you are right about this: you are a terribly trodden thing. Keep the landlord out of your mind. Until everything is upside down he will try to claw his way back to power any way he can. Beard the devil."

I wanted to take her advice. The typhoon had changed everything. As I waded through our yard, I found a raccoon hugging a tree, mummified with silver eyes, preserved by the stinging taste of the air. The marsh had become a sea forest, the trees turned mangroves, all bones no leaves. The nailed rats had teeny men carved out of their bodies as if by cookie cutter.

I splashed down what was once our driveway and saw the mansion. It had stranded on a sand bar, inhabited now only by birds. Ahead, translucent faces glided between the mangroves, soupy fog swirling during warm breezes. Unrecognizable limbs swung by moonlight.

Things had changed. Brackish children splashed through mist. The wheel that Shara spoke about was spinning, I believed in it, this ocean inverting all in its path. There was a rise and wane to everything.

"Hey!" shouted a shrill voice, startling me. "Look!"

A brackish boy knelt, nudging something washed up on the tracks. "Get away from that," I barked, voice raspy. It was a body, a wealthy person from the mansion, still wearing shiny dress shoes. A smaller person had been sliced out of the larger one, the absent head oversized for the gaping silhouette left in the torso.

"Want to play underwater? There's treasure." The brackish boy turned his waxen face on mine—the ruddy frown of a grown man—and I noticed his jerked meat arms before I screamed and he dove into the tumbling wake with a gleeful cry.

卌 卌 卌 卌卌 卌 |||

Shara kicked a clogged carpet downstairs. It slapped the water and scattered a school of red squid along with a predatory fish that made a V on the surface. "Open the front door," she said. "At this point it's holding water. Let's chase the fish back into the cellar."

We collaborated to herd fish, lobsters, squid, crabs, and eels toward the basement. Shara paddled the water sternly with a broom. Then she guarded the door while I scooped up starfish and sea cucumbers to toss into the lagoon below.

A great wave would hit us tonight. An underwater earthquake had cut a wall of water reaching the sky, so the word went. Shara's radio buzzed with hopefuls packing up their tents and trudging inland. The other brackish held steady, beholden to the landlord.

"I hope this wave turns out to be exaggerated," Shara murmured, nuzzling my shoulder. "If the house goes, we have no way out but the landlord."

"Let me scavenge," I said. "Maybe a canoe stranded."

She nodded, fastening a hat on my head. "Don't take long."

I promised to be quick. When I opened the door, water rushed out over the softened boards on the porch. The ocean had retreated in anticipation of the great wave. I could see it on the horizon—a blue mountain blending into the clouds.

I followed the railroad down to the exposed seafloor. A few vessels had sunken here, smashed to bones on Atlantis homes, but none were useable. Sagging anemones waited for their gods. Under an abandoned motorway, a barnacled railcar sat alone on the tracks, topped with a mop of seaweed. It was here I encountered the landlord.

"I told you," he murmured, not surprised to see me. "A train holding something precious is coming with the ocean. Here is my lobster, trapped on the seafloor, safe in the prison I made for him. Have you seen those fucking things in the night?"

I approached carefully, noticing a busted lock in one of his hands and a hammer in the other. The sliding door to the train carriage was open. "Yes. The children, we call them," I said. "I don't know what you did in life to deserve their attention, but you should leave. Let Shara alone and make for higher ground."

He looked at me sideways. "Shara . . . ." he said. I could see the unbidden images flashing through his mind of kissing her nipples or whatever it was he desired. Perhaps he wanted insight into the mysterious wheel. "They called me slumlord. They lived here in these Atlantis homes and I owned the whole beach. For my son, I bled them for every dollar."

I crept closer, peering over his shoulder. There was a dark shape sitting in the box.

"I didn't care when my tenants stopped having babies; they couldn't afford to feed them," he sighed. "Then I saw the first *child* run across the road. Next came the letters under my door. Photos of sleeping kids, rolled up in carpets, slumped over at the table, though of course they weren't asleep. Those letters were threats. No way would I let them take my son's birthright."

There were tears guttered in his cheeks. Now I could see the red scars and had no doubt they had come from the fingers of a tiny person. The skeleton in the train was frozen in a yawn; it had not been dissected like the other bodies, locked away as it was. "You did it," I realized. "You locked your son inside and pushed him into the sea."

"He was a divine creature," the landlord said. "Too soft for this business. He wouldn't have protected our fortune and so I protected him. Now I start over—I take a new wife and make a new son. Trust me, I'm doing you a favor."

I didn't have time to react as his hammer whistled through the air onto my head, but a black pit opened and the ground rushed to meet my chin. The hammer came down again and I saw my legs insect-jerking. My mind went warm, swamped with flickers before emptiness surrounded my final confused thought.

卌 卌 卌 卌 卌 卌 ||||

My body lay over the salty stones.

The landlord didn't bother to hide his crime.

The tsunami would wipe the place clean and he could ride into the future with Shara.

Uncanny figures peered around seaweed mats and from behind the wheels of the railcar. Children walking on the heels of their hands approached and touched me all over. A serrated saw rubbed my shoulders—a haunted object, the edge of a bone with holes drilled along its length.

First, they cut my head away from my arms in a straight line down toward my waist, leaving strips from my chest for arms and legs. I hardly cared about the tweaks of pain. The overwhelming sensation was of weight sloughing away, the stress of years gone. Like a snake peeling off a silvery sock of skin, it was the opposite of shedding, really, of *losing something*, because as strips of me fell away I gained in clarity.

With a final snap of sinew separating whittle from wood, I could see again. A jubilant, mischievous energy seized me. My limbs were ropey and light. We ran, all of us children, toward the wave. I recognized some—the rich kids who had vanished surfing. Others must have come from the Atlantis homes.

The wave will deliver something beautiful. The thought came to me unbidden as the other children, undead mouths stretching with wicked delight, raised their arms in thanks. A ship large as a town floated on the wave's crest, carried for miles. Its shape made a leviathan shadow. We would board and let it drift us over the world twice over.

I stopped suddenly, watching the other children plink into the wall of water. I no longer wanted to dive into the tsunami. What I wanted was—

The great wave swept my legs away, swirling me toward Shara, blasting bubbles through my rubber limbs which hooked on shingles and concrete chunks and car frames and other debris. I could pump my legs along the seafloor, and when I sucked in water I jetted forward by a hole in my cratered back.

My watery talents didn't end there. As I flew above the sand, I saw a wispy trail at head level, bubbles too fine for a normal eye to detect. When I extended an arm into this stream, I spun, caught by a current. Delighted, I leaned into the trail, shooting forward with the full force of the wave. A geyser of comfort warmed my chest when I neared the edge of our property. The feeling radiated from the mound where I had buried a tin of shark teeth days ago.

When I erupted from of the water, Shara was hoisting herself through a hole in the roof. The wave had blown out the windows and doors. She heaved up the still life, wrapped in paper to protect it from spray. The sight of her evoked a sensation I had never felt before—a mix of scent and gravity, pleasant but intense, drawing me toward her—I could only describe it as *UP*. I wanted to help her. She noticed me and smiled as if my carved body was of no concern.

"We need to leave," I said. "There's a safe place." Indeed, not far, the gunmetal ship loomed. It may have once housed planes for military operations, but now trees grew on its deck and ferns spilled over its side. But Shara had no way to get there.

"Look at this!" howled the landlord. He was weaving the motorboat toward us, wearing sunglasses and a painted grin. He'd dabbed concealer on the gouges left by his son. If Shara emitted *UP*, he emitted *DOWN*, and the air rippled around him—fire wicked his skin. I wanted to drag him into the water. He kept one hand on the wheel but the other hovered lower. He was concealing something behind the dashboard. He had passed three other tenants without picking them up. They yelled and waved in the distance.

"Go," Shara said sharply. "I don't know what happens if he catches you."

I scampered up the weathervane, desperate to find a piece of debris large enough to carry Shara. Nothing but a chair caught my eye, which wouldn't outrun a boat.

"Lucky girl," said the landlord, yards away. "You never gave me time of day, but here I am to rescue you. You won't be saying no to my company, not after a couple nights at sea."

He grasped for Shara. Then I saw them—the children, once inheritors of fortunes, gliding toward us, pushing surfboards. They'd retained their vessels after they'd died, delivering one final gift for Shara. I sprung from my perch, wrapping soaked arms around the landlord's head.

He tore at my back. I hung on with rodeo joy. Shara knelt on a surfboard and paddled for her life. A dozen underwater hands shoved the landlord's motorboat aboard the roof, where the propeller shattered. He was stranded.

With a pop, I had lost: he held me helpless in his arms. Milky eyes fixed on the face of the boy he had killed once already. They grew shiny till they dribbled down his cheeks, settling in his scars. "I didn't want her to leave," he wept. In the belly of the boat, I saw what he'd been hiding—a leghold trap.

"My son, I flew too close to the sun," he said. "I'm sorry. I burn while I look for a way out of this ocean of grief. I deserve this. Go ahead—kill me! Turn me child as they did you!"

I twisted out of his hands and slithered into the water without a word. I cast a look back and caught his mournful gaze disappearing in a blaze. It was true he'd earned his fate. He'd spend his days trodden as an insect, and nobody would give him the gift they'd given me.

I caught Shara easily and crawled onto her craft. She balanced the painting on her hip as she rowed. "The still life is to remember you by," she told me. "You've changed. But what you've become is *still life*. More life than you ever had before. We must remember that."

She was right. My back was free from tension. When I gazed over our churning world, I only felt a sense of endless time for watching clams tuck themselves into sand, the freedom to pluck salted berries from the swamp, reliance on the beautiful sun. The thing about the canvas in Shara's arms was that though the faces had been carved into apples, those children were no less present than if they'd been hanging on our surfboard. I'd be there too.

James Cato is an environmental organizer in Pittsburgh where he lives with his pet gecko, Bocci. Look for his writing in *SmokeLong Quarterly*, *The Forge*, and *Daily Science Fiction*, among other places. He tweets humbly @the_sour_potato and his work lives on jamescatoauthor.com/fiction. His first collection, *Becoming Roadkill*, is out now at Red Bird Chapbooks.

A Shape that Has No Name

Monica Wendel

Of course the planes weren't going to explode on their way to JFK. But we liked watching them just in case.

"Don't you remember on 9-11, how they said that the buildings were bombed?" King asked.

"You remember 9-11?" King had that look in his green eyes, dreamy yet determined, that I'd known since high school. The look when he declared that mushrooms were fertilized by dead fish, and therefore were not vegetarian, much less vegan. Or the look when he announced that the Ant Liberation Front (ALF) was responsible for the release of Mr. Murphy's ant colonies.

King turned to face me, leaning on his side. "I remember 9-11. I remember tons of stuff from that age. When I was two I fell down the stairs and peed blood in my diaper. I remember my mom changing it."

I didn't believe him, but I liked pretending. "There's another one," I said, pointing at the sky.

The plane was low, and in the early morning light its belly looked soft and pink as a puppy's. King took my hand as I lifted it, and pinned it gently to the roof. The black tar held April's warmth. I knew what he wanted: he wanted to fuck one more time before the sun came up. He liked racing against time, running late, and he liked almost being caught.

But King didn't ask me to have sex. He held my hand and looked at me for a long time as we listened to an ambulance call down Flushing Ave on the way to Woodhull Hospital. We had been up all night together, and his eyes were as pink as the bellies of the planes. I listened to the unguarded silence the siren left behind, and wondered what he was seeing. Then King spoke. "Belle, do you want to come to Marion with me?"

That was the thing about King. On the J train he put his hands up my skirt, and in the Chicken Hut he wanted me to touch him by the wall while everyone else danced to Big Freida. And when I didn't want to he told me about the girls who did want to, who had done it, at some point in college or high school, way before we started: Katie and Olivia, Meredith and the other Belle. He liked telling me how good it was with them. Which was why he wanted to do it with me. "Who's Marion?"

"Illinois. Where Darius is," he said, his face hardening at the sound of his brother's name.

"The jail?"

"The prison."

"Oh," I said, searching his face and trying to understand why he was asking me. "Umm, I don't know. When?"

King leaned over me and checked his phone. "He's being released in six weeks, and it's a two-day drive. We'd leave on May 20th."

"I can't," I said, relieved. "I have my final teaching practicum then."

"So do it online," King said, loosening his grip on my hand.

"The schools will be open by then," I said. "Right? I'm pretty sure I'll have to go in. Do you want to ask, like, Tatiana?" Tatiana was my roommate, and besides being prettier than me, she was also much, much smarter.

"Maybe, Belle." He checked something on his phone. "It could be, you know. Kind of an adventure."

I took a breath and tried to connect myself to him. My head never worked right around King; I was too swept up in the ocean of him. We'd met in high school and orbited each other for years, never quite part of the same friend group. I'd see his green eyes across a flood of people in the cafeteria and something deep inside me would bend; water shaping itself over the continental shelf. "Maybe," I said. "Are you sure it wouldn't be weird?"

"Why would it be weird?" King pulled his shirt on. "I should get going."

"Okay." Another siren sang down Flushing. It felt like they never stopped. "I'll see you later."

King left, and I logged onto Google Classroom. My students didn't have the resources to log on to the classroom at certain times, so everything was asynchronous.

There wasn't much to do. Yesterday, in the bitterness of isolation, I had made a week's worth of worksheets and uploaded them. I'd also made a video about how to make an abstract drawing and uploaded it to YouTube and Google Classroom. It wasn't clear if any of them had watched it. If they even could watch it.

How long would this last? I looked out the window onto the driveway, feeling inside me the loneliness that only the classroom took away. There was a buzzing warmth to elementary schools, to kids, that I couldn't find anywhere else.

And so I missed the kids—not just missed them, but missed them, physically. I missed their skinny arms and the way their bellies paunched out. I missed the way they couldn't say "R"s, and I missed the way they talked while they ate, with their hands pinwheeling and their eyes growing huge with concentration.

But I didn't have any theory to back up my feelings. King, Tatiana, the people they introduced me to—they all stood for something. They all had purpose. They believed in anarchofeminism, and ecoprimitivism; they knew the intricacies of squatting. They could tell you what was wrong, and their theories could explain why, and then they had a solution. Meanwhile, I was scrounging for new markers and debating the best size of crayons for three-year-old fingers. I was wiping muffin crumbs off sticky faces and giving hugs. I didn't know if I was fixing any problems or making them worse; I didn't know if I was showing kids love or teaching them how to obey a fucked-up institution.

The closest I came to believing in something was believing in King. Following him into dumpsters. Helping him organize fund-raisers for his brother. Serving drinks at the performance space at the John Bosch House.

Tatiana interrupted my wallowing. "Hey," she said, leaning against the door. "You working right now?"

I looked at the screen. The cursor blinked on an empty Google Doc. My whole fucking life depended on Google. "I don't know," I said. "I was thinking about making a podcast that the kids could listen to."

"Come to my office with me," Tatiana said, her Russian accent as crisp as my parents'. "I'm going to 3D print masks."

I stared at her for a second. She wore all black and dyed her dirty blonde hair black, too. But you wouldn't know that unless you lived with her. I was the only one who saw her roots. "Seriously?"

She nodded. "Hammer is providing us with the supplies. You can use his bike because it has a trailer. We'll ride the plastics there, print them using the code, and give them to Woodhull."

I looked at her and blinked, wondering, for a moment, what it would be like to be heroic. To be Hammer and know how to steal from Home Depot. To be Tatiana and know how to 3D print masks. To be King and drive across the continent to pick up Darius. To be anyone, anybody, but myself. "Are we taking the Williamsburg Bridge or the Manhattan?"

"Williamsburg," she said.

"Sure," I said, closing out of the Google Doc. "Just let me get dressed."

We called our house the John Bosch House because of some tiled lettering on the front stoop, but it was really two houses. The main house had seven bedrooms over three floors, a classic Brooklyn brownstone. We lived in the garage behind and to the side of it, Tatiana and I upstairs, and Hammer downstairs, next to the performance space. Before the pandemic, it had felt like one house. In the mornings, I would leave my door open before leaving to student teach, and Hammer would come in at 6 am, just as he was coming home. We took turns bringing home dumpstered juice and Whole Foods treats.

But with the pandemic, we had cleaved. Or maybe I had.

Tatiana and I unlocked our bikes from the performance space and pushed off down Willoughby Avenue. We rode slowly, pacing ourselves, pulling the heavy supplies on trailers on our bikes. The Williamsburg Bridge crested, and without speaking, we nodded at each other and stopped at the top.

The J train passed by, rattling the bridge. I hoped no one else would be riding near us. What if someone came too close and we breathed in their air? Below, the water was choppy and green; above, the sky gray and damp.

Tatiana took out a water bottle, and I checked my phone. We had one downhill to get to Delancey, then it was flat crosstown, then the hills of the Upper West Side, then Tatiana's office at Columbia. Tatiana noticed me looking at my phone. "Did you see what King posted?" she asked.

"No," I said, my stomach sinking. I opened up Instagram. *Photo dump*, his caption read. I scrolled through the ten photos. There were the bare branches of the tree you could see from outside my window, not filtered black-and-white, but looking desaturated in a cloudy sky. Empty Times Square.

And Tatiana.

Tatiana on the other side of a dumpster, their hands reaching for the same apple. Tatiana on our roof, staring up at the planes. A screenshot of Tatiana facilitating a prison support Zoom meeting. I swiped right, and right again. Finally, I appeared on the last slide—our ankles, tangled together. "When did you guys hang out on the roof?"

Tatiana put her phone away and closed her water bottle. "I'm not sure. It might have been when you were in Florida."

Fucking Florida. I had my cousin's wedding in West Palm Beach in February, during midwinter break. "Oh, that's cool." My hands were shaking. I rubbed them on my shorts and stared at the holes in my black tights.

"Is it, though?" Tatiana laughed. "We went to the fundraiser at the Knockdown Center. It took forever to get back. The bus never came, and we had to walk the whole way home."

I looked down at the East River. King must have slept over; where else would he have slept? But did he sleep on the floor, or in Tatiana's bed?

It always felt easy to distance myself from my body while having sex with King. It felt better that way. He was attentive, but also precise; I couldn't help feeling, while we were having sex, that I could be anyone; that the basic anatomy was the same from person to person, and what he was doing wasn't so different.

But sleeping in bed together felt different. That was when I could look at him and see him vulnerable, his eyelids turning purple-ish. The moments when he didn't have to be King of anything. It took a long time before he fell asleep with me. I loved the gentleness of his breathing, and how he slept with his arms crossed, as though he were covering himself.

The thought of him having sex with Tatiana was not so bad. I had already accepted it. But the thought of him sleeping in bed with her felt like a betrayal.

I kicked the pedal of Hammer's bike and watched it spin in the air, moving but going nowhere. "I might go to Illinois with him. To pick up his brother from prison."

Tatiana nodded slowly. "You better prepare yourself. Prison is another world."

"I know," I said, even though I didn't.

She leaned over the bridge. "What about your students?"

I laughed an empty laugh. It sounded more like a cough, which then, of course, freaked me out. "I didn't just cough," I said. The waters lapped at the feet of the bridge. "I haven't really been able to get in touch with them. They're too young to have laptops or phones. Some of them have tablets. There's not really much you can do through a screen."

"You just seem so happy when you're teaching." For some reason her accent kicked in strong, and each syllable was musical. "Is there any other way you can connect with them?"

"I don't know." And it felt, then, like my students had sailed off somewhere, had been abandoned. That I had abandoned them. I shook my head. "Yeah, maybe. I'll try to figure something out." I put my foot on the pedal. "Wanna keep riding?"

"The *world* won't end," said King. "Humans will end."

We were in a lush Pennsylvania hollow, one of those places where the Allegheny mountains dip into valley. "You don't think that humans will destroy the earth?" I asked. The green outside was encompassing but fragile, a mist that might dissolve at any moment.

King scoffed at this. "With any luck, humans will kill each other and the dolphins will take over."

"Unless we kill all the dolphins first." I gazed at his profile. "Wait, really? You think the world will be okay?"

"If you were on a life raft, and it was you and a cow and two other people, who would you throw off the life raft?"

I knew this was a trick question. "The cow."

"See?" He thumped the steering wheel with his hand. "But the cow won't kill anyone. The people on the life raft would kill animals. The cow wouldn't."

"That's true," I said. "So do you not like people?"

He shrugged. "I don't think their lives are worth more than any other lives."

The rolling hills were making me nauseated—that, and I was expecting my period. Today, or if not today, tomorrow. We'd been on the road now for five hours and we were making terrible time. First, King was late picking me up. Then he wanted to see the field hospital set up in Central Park. Then we hit construction outside of

Harrisburg. “I have to puke.”

“Again?”

Right. That was the other thing making us late.

The car rumbled to the side of the road, and I sprinted out to the tree line. Only bile was left in my stomach. I sat down, dizzy, and took a sip of ginger ale. Tears came to my eyes, but I brushed them away. I was supposed to be helping King, not having him take care of me.

My hands shook. I felt like shit.

“You okay?” King asked when I made it back to the car.

I nodded. “Sorry.”

“It’s okay,” he said, but his voice was flat.

He pulled out onto I-76, and I willed my stomach to calm down. “What were we talking about?”

“I dunno,” he said, chewing his lip, suddenly looking worried.

“I’m sorry,” I said again. “It’s just—I haven’t been in a car in a long time—and—”

“It’s not that.” He took his hat off and put it on the dashboard.

“Oh,” I said, wondering, then what it was.

“Did you know that Darius has a job already?”

It was weird to hear King call his brother Darius. This whole time, he’d existed as part of King, like one of King’s limbs—or a phantom limb. Missing but felt. Always present, but invisible. “Wasn’t that part of his release? Like the condition of release?”

King’s face was tight and twisted. “He’s doing PR for the ACLU.”

“Isn’t that—isn’t that—” I took a sip of ginger ale. “I mean, isn’t that a good thing?”

“It’s not fair,” said King.

“Of course not,” I said, reassuringly. “He should never have been in prison.”

“Not that.” King sped up and passed a double tractor trailer. “That now he has a job. And I’m still stuck in the same place I’ve always been.”

“You want a job?”

“He’s coming out of prison and he’s got a support network, he’s got people rooting for him, he’s got me coming to pick him up. And I’ve spent the last three years making all that happen. What do I have to show for it? Nothing.”

I thought back to the benefit show I had helped King put on in the performance space. Booking bands, buying alcohol, counting bills at the end of the night. And that was on top of King's GoFundMe. "You've done so much for him."

"My parents' house is double mortgaged to pay for his lawyer. They do everything for him. And I'm expected to do more."

"I'm sorry," I said, lamely.

"Sometimes I wonder what my life would look like if it had been me in prison."

"Are you . . . jealous? That he's in jail?"

I didn't mean for my tone to sound accusatory, but King grew silent, a silence I could only read as anger. Finally he spoke. "I thought you'd understand, Belle." We rolled over more hills. "And it's prison, not jail."

"I'm sorry."

"Stop apologizing."

I didn't know what to say to that. There was nothing to say. I looked out for a signpost, any sign, besides mile markers. I remembered when the feds were first investigating Darius. They subpoenaed all the electronics in King's house, so he lost his laptop our senior year of high school. He had to write his papers in the library. He never told me that; I found it out through friends.

And that was how all the information came. Rumors, drips, texts. Sometimes facts drifted to the surface: an article in NPR about Darius's case and what it meant for the Earth First! movement, or King quoted in the New York Times about his brother's gentle nature.

"If I had been in prison instead of him, what would we be?"

"What would . . . who be?"

"Us," said King. "Would we be together?"

I stared out the window, but the mountains gave me no answers. Were we together now? But I knew what he meant. He wasn't my partner, but he wasn't my nothing, either. We were something, even if we hadn't defined it. I tried to picture myself organizing a GoFundMe, planning a concert fundraiser, posting pictures and updates from prison. I tried to picture myself being that person—King's person. I tried to picture myself and King together without his physical presence. Without sleeping in bed together, and waking up together. Without his fingers on my thigh, and my hands reaching.

Would I have waited for him? For how long?

Would I go three years without sex? Would I schedule my life around his phone calls? Would I go to Marion, IL every other month to see him for a few hours two days in a row?

I glanced over at King, his olive skin and strong features. His parents were outsiders in Belle Harbor, Persian Jews who somehow didn't make it over the Gil Hodges Bridge to Brooklyn. My parents, the few times they saw him, asked me if he was an Arab. I decided to lie. "Yeah," I said. "You'd be getting sick of me sending you letters," I joked. "And books."

King relaxed into the seat cushions. Then he reached out and took my hand as I asked him to pull over, once again.

That night, King wanted to have sex in the hotel room, but I was spotting. "It's light," I said, relieved.

"I don't care," he said.

And then he was bloody, and I pretended it was my first time.

King fell asleep, and I touched the blood that had flowed out from me when we had sex. It didn't look like normal period blood. *Have my period but the blood looks weird*, I googled. Nothing about pregnancy came up. So I was probably not pregnant. I put my phone away and looked at King's face.

The first time I slipped into a dumpster with King, I couldn't believe the sense of possibility. Here was capitalism, wealth; here were $8 juices still sealed. And just beyond, I could make out the Manhattan skyline.

If he had been in prison, not Darius, then I would have a sense of purpose, I thought. I would know what was right and what was wrong. Because right now, I couldn't figure it out. I wasn't an ecoprimitivist; I didn't want a world where kids died from cancer because we were against technology. And I wasn't an anarchist; hadn't Occupy Wall Street dissolved? Some of the older activists had been part of that, and when they talked about it, I wondered, if it was so wonderful, so powerful, why it hadn't changed anything. Why we weren't doing it again.

And I wasn't a socialist, either. Because the services that were supposed to help my students hurt them—like the homeless shelters, and ACS. In Bed-Stuy, when I saw those wheat pasted black signs that said *they separate kids from their parents in Brooklyn, too*—I found myself nodding. Fuck liberalism. Fuck the idea that the government is going to help you.

But who was I if I didn't believe in anything? It made me nothing. A shadow of King. A sidekick. A housewife in training decorating a Pinterest-ready classroom.

King rolled over in his sleep, and I looked at his body. I felt addicted to it, wanting him even as he slept. Was my emptiness how he liked me—why he liked me? Maybe this was the answer. He could fill me, over and over again, and pour me out, and I would fit the shapes that he wanted.

I went to the bathroom. The blood was already gone. I tried not to think about what that meant. If it meant anything at all.

"Sir, I cannot let you in." The prison guard slapped King's driver's license down. "This license expired two years ago." Her mask hung loosely around her chin.

King's jaw set. I watched a vein pop out of his forehead. "We need to secure his release."

"Sir." The word was a whole sentence, saying everything. "I cannot release Inmate 56835 to you without a valid form of identification. If you cannot provide me with identification, there is nothing that I can do."

"I have something," I said. "I have ID."

The guard swung her head slowly. "Ma'am, you are not on the approved list."

King scrolled through his phone. "Here is a copy of my passport," he said, holding the phone up to the plexiglass barrier.

The guard's eyes flickered over the screen. "I cannot accept a copy of a ID. You need the original."

King's eyes bored into hers. "We drove two days to get here."

"I'm sorry to hear that, sir." She did not sound sorry.

"Is there any way I can get on the approved list?" I asked. King rolled his eyes. I guess I said something dumb.

The guard almost looked sympathetic. "Ma'am, the list needed to be submitted six weeks in advance in order for the Department of Corrections to run the necessary background check."

"So what now?" King broke in.

The guard looked at me, and I tried to look as harmless as possible. "If no one is authorized for the release, then Darius will depart today in a prison van for the Greyhound Station and will be provided with a ticket to his destination as well as $40 to cover incidentals."

"Thank you," I said. "I really appreciate it."

King visibly flinched. "Where's the Greyhound Station?"

"It's fine," I said, touching his arm. "I can find it on my phone."

"You have a blessed day, ma'am," said the guard. "Next!"

We walked out of the prison into the blistering sunlight. Endless fields stretched around us, the earth made industrial. Monotonous fields of corn and alfalfa. Feed for animals, fertilized by—by what? Some chemical brew from Monsanto. I hated the Midwest. I searched on my phone. "Here," I said, pushing my phone into King's hands. "The Greyhound Station is only a ten minute drive. We can go there and wait for your brother."

King dropped his head into his hands. "Fuck. Fuck!" He kicked a tire.

"It's okay," I said. "Look. We'll go to the bus station. It can't be that big. We'll find Darius. We'll bring him the food we brought. And we'll drive straight home."

King spoke through clenched teeth. "You mean drop him off at the halfway house."

"Yeah. Exactly. And the halfway house is right near my place. So you'll be able to see him . . . whenever." I shook the brown bag we had, which unfortunately sounded like I was shaking treats at a dog. "His food is right here. He'll be really happy to see us."

"This better work, Belle."

How is this my fault? "We don't have another choice."

At the Greyhound Station, we waited, we waited, we waited. I stood outside, hoping that sunlight killed Covid, trying not to think of the crowded air of the prison van. And then the van appeared, and I ran inside and grabbed King, and he ran out.

The men filed out of the vehicle wearing nondescript clothes. The clothes they came in with—blue jeans, t-shirts, some of them carrying sweatshirts and winter coats, wearing Timberland Boots. They were mixed, some Black, some white, some Hispanic, some looking Middle Eastern. And then King took a step forward, and there was Darius. They hugged, and I glimpsed his face before it disappeared into the warmth of King's shoulder.

The hug lasted too long. King was supporting Darius.

Darius lifted his face, and King spoke. "Darius, this is my friend, Belle. She drove with me."

"Hi," I said, waving one hand a little bit.

Darius nodded at me. His face looked like King's, but white and gaunt while King's was olive and filled out. His breathing was shallow, open-mouthed. "I remember you." His neck strained. It took a moment for him to fill his lungs with air to breathe out his words. "You wrote me letters from the tree."

"Umm, no," I said. "That wasn't me."

He nodded again, and King steered him towards the car. "Here's some food, man."

Darius looked inside approvingly. "This looks great. Thanks."

But he didn't eat any. He sat in the car and put the bag by his feet, then leaned his head back.

We drove east. Sometimes Darius coughed. There was a strange energy in the car. I had expected to feel love, warmth, closeness, gratitude—something big, something to fill up the space. Instead the car felt more empty. This was it? This was their reunion?

"Just let me know if you want to stop, man," said King.

"Thanks," said Darius. And then they were silent for another five miles, punctuated only by Darius's coughs.

"We were planning on driving straight through," King said, breaking the silence.

"Sure," said Darius.

From the backseat, I tried to see Darius's breathing. And then I couldn't stand it anymore. "Darius," I asked through my mask, "do you have Covid?"

He shrugged. "I got sick about a month ago. The doctor gave me some cough drops. I didn't take them, though. They contained honey."

"And—you've been sick this whole time?" King was trying to make eye contact with me in the rearview mirror, but I resisted. Darius didn't say anything. "Darius, can you breathe?"

He gave a depressing chuckle.

Now I found King's eyes. "King, maybe we should go to the hospital."

King tightened his grip on the wheel. "No."

"Why?"

Darius spoke. "Belle, it's really nice of you." He paused to breathe. "I don't have health insurance."

"So what?" I said. "It's your *life*."

"Hospitals are just there to make money," said King. "They don't do anything except watch you die."

"King, my mom is a doctor."

He paused, then said icily, "Don't you think that proves my point?"

I flinched. "Fuck you."

"You don't know what you're talking about."

"I do about this," I said. "Darius, you need help."

"I'm fine," he mumbled.

"See?" said King. "He's fine."

"He's not fine."

Still the fields swooshed past us. My hands were shaking. "King, he can't breathe. Millions of people are dying from Covid. Okay, maybe not millions. But you've heard the sirens. He needs to see a doctor."

"You think he's going to see a doctor in the hospital, Belle? No. He's going to die in the waiting room just like all those other people."

"Not if we go to the hospital here. If we wait until we get back to the city, yeah, that might happen. But the hospitals here are empty."

"I'm not going to drop my brother off to die somewhere."

Darius shook his head back and forth. "Guys, guys. Let's not fight."

"Fine. Let's stop at a CVS."

"What's a CVS going to do?"

A pulse oximeter, I thought. A thermometer. A pharmacist who can call an ambulance, and then he'll have no choice but to go. "I have to puke," I declared, and the car screeched to the shoulder.

Okay. I actually didn't, this time. But I walked away from the car towards a field of alfalfa that smelled like burning and leaned down. I waited, hoping that this would work. And eventually it did, because King came out. "You okay, Belle?"

I wiped my face and looked up at him. "Yeah. Are you mad at me?"

"Why do you always think I'm mad at you?" His hand reached for my side; I curved into it. I was watery near him. I leaned into the pressure there, about to apologize, but stopped. We kissed, and I hoped he couldn't taste my lie. "I love you," he whispered. His hands moved over my waist and hips, and I looped my fingers around the back of his neck, making a net that would keep him near me. "I love you too," I whispered.

"Listen. I know you're worried about Darius. He's going to be okay."

I looked towards the car as though I could see something there. Of course I couldn't. "King, what if we get to the halfway house and they don't let him in? Then he'll have to go to Woodhull."

"That's not going to happen, Belle." He hooked a finger between my shirt and jeans, let it rest on the bare skin. If I was water, he was lightning, and together we were an ocean made electric. "Trust me."

I sometimes hated King, and sometimes loved King, but I always, always wanted to fuck King. I searched his face for the answer to the question I hadn't asked, the question my body was asking. He closed his eyes and kissed me again. Every time we had sex—no, every time we kissed—no, every time he looked at me—I thought it was going to be the last time. I thought there would never be another moment, ever again. This time, when we kissed, his hand unbuttoned my pants, and I leaned into him, like a ship opening to salt water. Something breaking, something beautiful, and then a storm.

We walked back to the car together, hip to hip. Darius was sprawled out in the backseat, his head leaning back against the window. "You okay?" I asked him.

He gave a silent thumbs up.

"Mind if I drive?" I asked King.

"I should probably drive."

I looked at Darius, but his eyes were closed. "What about your brother?"

"What do you mean?"

"I'll drive and you can help him," I said, getting into the front seat before King could stop me.

I pulled out from the shoulder and onto the road. King dozed in the front seat: like always, I was energized after orgasm, while he was sleepy. There had to be a hospital somewhere. Didn't farmers get injured all the time? Losing fingers, chemical burns, stuff like that? I wished I knew something, anything.

The road unspooled before us, humming and empty. Straight and flat. We were nowhere. I drove ten, fifteen, twenty miles, waiting for a sign for a hospital, and then, when there was no sign, waiting for a sign for an exit. There was only the humming of the road. And then there was more humming, because my phone was buzzing. "Hey Tatiana," I said, pressing the buttons on the car's audio screen. "You're on speakerphone."

King shook himself awake.

"How's it going?" she asked. It was always strange hearing American-isms in her Russian accent, the same way I felt when I heard my father say "like" in a sentence.

King glanced into the backseat. I watched concern flicker over his face—the first moments of remembering where we were and realizing that things might not be okay. "We got Darius," he said.

"Is it okay for me to post an update for the GoFundMe?" Tatiana asked.

"Sure," said King.

There was an awkward silence. "What do you want it to say?" Tatiana prodded. I could practically see her in her room in Brooklyn, fingers poised over the keyboard.

"*We're on our way home with Darius,*" I said. "*Thanks for all your support?*"

"Sure," said Tatiana. "Send a picture over, too."

New pictures meant more shares, which meant more posts, which meant more funds. I looked in the rearview mirror. Darius had not stirred. "Darius? Darius, are you awake?"

His shoulders lifted as he tried to breathe: a gasping inhale, then exhale.

"Thanks, Tatiana," King said, then hung up.

"Why'd you hang up?"

"Why'd you try to wake up Darius?"

"He's not even in good enough shape for us to take a picture of him. And I'm supposed to pretend everything is fine?"

"No one is asking you to pretend anything, Belle. Why do you feel like you always have to pretend?"

I kept my hands steady. "Look, I'm getting off at the next exit. Darius needs help."

King turned in the passenger's seat and reached his hand out to Darius. "Darius, how are you doing, man? You okay?"

"Don't bring me—to the hospital—" Darius exhaled.

The fields moved past, monotonous, green, unnamed. "You're really sick, Darius," I said. "We're trying to help you."

"Don't leave me," he said. I tore my eyes from the road and met his in the rearview mirror and nearly hit a discarded, shredded-up tire.

"Sorry!" I yelped. Uncertainty spun within me as fast as the car's wheels. "Darius, what about urgent care? They won't keep you there."

We passed some white low-slung buildings: egg farming. I tried not to think of the horrors contained within, the birds birthing, over and over again, pushing out almost-life ceaselessly, white moons dropping from their bodies. King spoke. "They can't cure Covid. They won't do anything there."

Straight ahead through the windshield: a brilliant sky, aching with spring. Below: the unceasing green fields that at first glance are beautiful, but, closer, are another factory, industrial corn and alfalfa, poisoned earth, poisoned leaves, poisoned insects, poisoned weeds, poisoned farmers—and us, in the hermetically sealed car, breathing in Darius's poisoned breath. The unnatural landscape, natural disease. Or was it the other way around?

And suddenly, there it was. I was in danger. King was in danger. And—was there—in me—also in danger—

"We have to go to CVS," I said. "I need a pregnancy test."

King leapt up so quickly that the car tilted, his strength unbalancing our metal and rubber ship sailing across the continent. But he said nothing as I took the next exit, pulled to the shoulder, and googled *pharmacy locations* as the corn waved at us in its loneliness.

It turns out you don't pee on the stick. You're supposed to pee in a cup and put the stick in it. Just another way the media has lied to us!

While I waited, I checked my texts. *Send picture for update when you can,* Tatiana wrote. There were also Instagram notifications and an email from my professor confirming that my student teaching practicum was submitted. *I hope this email finds you well.*

In these trying times. . . . I scrolled past it.

I took my phone out and took a picture of the pee cup with the stick in it and sent it to Tatiana. *Not for update. :(*, I wrote.

She called immediately. "Are you pregnant?"

I was sitting on the bathroom floor of a Starbucks while Darius and King waited in the car. Neither stubborn boy would agree to urgent care, but I got them to at least stop at a CVS, where we bought Acetaminophen for Darius's fever and a humidifier for his cough. A humidifier that could do absolutely nothing in a car. I scooted my butt closer to the cup and tried to peer in. "Yeah," I said, poking at the stick. "I see a line." I waited for that feeling to come back, the feeling in the car with the open sky and the knowing, but I didn't feel anything.

"You'll be okay," Tatiana said. "Do they have Plan B there?"

I dumped the pee in the toilet and flushed. "Hold on a sec," I said, and took a picture of the stick. The line was really pink—more magenta. Did that mean something? Then I threw that out, too. "Sorry, I couldn't hear you."

"Belle—" I could see her running her hands through her hair, twisting it up, her nervous habit, "whose is it?"

"What do you mean?" I asked, turning on the water. "It's mine."

A Russian curse on the other end of the line, then laughing. And then I was laughing, too, and crying.

"Belle! This is why you do not use dumpstered condoms. No. More. Dumpster. Condoms."

I couldn't tell if I was crying because I was laughing or laughing because I was crying. "Do you really think that King gets his condoms from a dumpster?"

"Probably! From where else would he get them?"

"I don't know. The store?" I wiped my nose on the back of my wrist. "I guess I always figured that he shoplifted them."

"And you're not on birth control."

It was half a question and half a statement. I thought about trying to explain to Tatiana how precarious all of it felt. My relationship with King. If it was even a relationship. Which it was not. How I was afraid that if I took any step towards him, the whole edifice would shatter. And so going on birth control would have come too close to promising myself that it would happen again.

That each time wasn't the last time. "I just figured that . . . like that it wouldn't . . . I don't know. I didn't know he would still . . . ." I swallowed. "Birth control takes like a month to work."

"Mmm," Tatiana murmured. "Well . . . now you're fucked."

"I know!" I said, wiping tears from my face. "What the fuck!"

Tatiana dissolved into riotous laughter.

I smiled at the face I saw in the mirror, blurry with tears. "Hold on. I have to wash my face."

"I'll get Plan B for you at the pharmacy," Tatiana said. "You don't need a prescription."

"Thanks. Yeah it would be a pain to get it here." Someone knocked on the door. "I have to get going. I miss you."

"Wait," she said. "How many weeks pregnant are you?"

"Umm, I was supposed to get my period yesterday. So that makes me . . . two weeks pregnant?"

"Let me check," she said. "That doesn't sound right." I stared at the door. "Belle, you're four weeks pregnant."

"No I'm not," I said. I pulled up the calendar on my phone. "I had my period four weeks ago."

"You start counting from the first day of your last period," she said. "I'm reading it on WebMD."

I started laughing again. "I hate this," I said. "Okay. So can I still take PlanB?" I wiped a few more tears from my eyes, and then I started crying a lot.

"Let me look this up. I don't think so. I'll call you back."

"Thanks," I said, wiping the tears away. I wasn't sobbing or anything like that. Just a lot of water everywhere, running down my face into my chest and shirt, snot on my sleeves. And then, even though it was so, so, gross, I slid down until I was lying on my back on the tile floor. I put my thumbs in my belly button and pointed my index fingers down to my legs, and I felt my hands on my body and imagined what was growing inside me.

It's not like I was struggling with a choice. That would mean that I had a decision to make. But there was no decision: I'd have to get rid of it. I just couldn't put it in the words I knew. It didn't feel like reproductive freedom. It didn't feel like control over my own body. It felt, instead, like someone had made the choice for me by ensuring that I wouldn't be eligible for paid time off until I'd worked a certain amount of months. And that daycare was too expensive. The world I lived in didn't want me to have a baby, and so I wouldn't have it. I breathed in and felt my low belly rise and fall, and I cried a little more for the poppy seed inside me, splitting and growing and splitting and growing. "I'm sorry," I said to it. It didn't matter if it was alive or not. You can love something that's not alive. You can love your future.

And then I realized that there was still one life I had left to save. One life, that is, besides my own.

I carried some ice water back to the car for King and Darius. "Sorry I took so long," I said. "It's positive."

"Congratulations," said Darius, at the same time King said "Oh, wow," and took his hat off.

"Crazy, huh?" I said, plopping next to King, who was sitting in the driver's seat. "I'll take care of it when we get back."

"Do you need me to do anything?" asked King. He looked worried.

"No, that's okay. Tatiana is going to—" King's expression froze me. "What?"

"Tatiana?"

The car suddenly felt very hot. It was too much to look at King, so I looked at Darius. "Yeah. Umm. She called while I was in the bathroom. So . . . ."

"You told Tatiana before you told me?"

The pain in King's voice thudded. "I—" The truth was, it hadn't even crossed my mind to tell King first. *Whose is it?* Tatiana had asked, not knowing that I was sleeping with King, and my dumbass answer: *It's mine*. "I'm sorry. I'm such a dumbass."

"Fucking shit, Belle! I'm not calling you a dumbass."

"It's yours," I said. "Like, it's definitely yours."

"What are you talking about? Of course it's mine. Who else's would it possibly be?"

"We shouldn't be having this conversation," I said, desperate to stay in the parking lot, but also desperate to escape. "I'm going to have an abortion as soon as I can."

"You're going to kill it?" King got out of the car and walked away. He wiped his face and stared at the sky as though drinking in the blue.

And then the sirens came. Slow at first, far away. They pulled into the parking lot. I climbed out of the car and waved my arms, directing them over. "Here," I said, when the EMTs came out. "This is Darius Kneiger. He's having trouble breathing."

King followed behind the ambulance while I stayed at the Starbucks, drinking an oat milk latte and drawing. My pen followed the same instructions I'd given my students, that abstract drawing video I'd posted in another lifetime, and for the first time, I listened to my own voice.

Look: here's a room of bubbles. A room of poppy seeds. A room of triangles, of rectangles, of squares, of hearts.

I call him King; his parents named him Eric Kneiger. Two names for the same life.

Here's a shape that has no name. And another, and another.

Here's a map of my pain. Here is my body, here is my phone. Here is the Communist Manifesto and Adam Smith. A Modest Proposal of tiny bodies. There's my father's green card; there's my mother's asylum application. The seas rise around Belle Harbor. The virus sweeps the streets of New York City until they empty.

This whole time, I had been thinking that I needed a theory to make sense of the world, thinking that I couldn't decide anything. But I'd forgotten that existing was an action. The act of living can be a rebellion.

For a long time I sat, letting the pen lead my hand. Letting the ink decide what to draw. I wondered if Darius wanted his life saved. If King did. I touched the drawing. But the only answers there were the ones I created. The only place I would be able to find an answer was the place inside myself.

Monica Wendel is interested in environmental writing, collaborations with visual artists, and pedagogy (in roughly that order). She holds an MFA from NYU, where she was awarded Goldwater and Starworks teaching fellowships. An associate professor at St. Thomas Aquinas College, her work has been published in the *Bellevue Literary Review*, *Rattle*, *Ploughshares*, and other journals. You can find her online at www.monicawendel.com.

"A Shape that Has No Name" originally appeared in the anthology *Our Magical Pandemic: Stories of Love and Whimsy in Lockdown.*

The Donor

Bernie Jean Schiebeling

The donor—Cleo—lived in one of those Seattle neighborhoods where you couldn't rent basement units anymore, so Sylvie pulled her clear plastic overshoes over her loafers before she even got out of her Uber. On the sidewalk, brackish water that smelled of mud and seaweed sloshed over her toes. The grinding whirr of industrial sump pumps rumbled up through her calves. With one arm drawn over her leather messenger bag, she splashed up the front steps to the unlatched front door and looked down the drizzly street to where the Uber's taillights were disappearing behind twin arches of water. No point pretending to hit the buzzer, then. She ducked inside.

A few moments later, she stood in front of a particle-board apartment door peppered with nail holes, the ghosts of festive wreaths. First she took a deep breath. Then she smiled. Now she knocked. A dog answered in the kind of baying barks that all ran together—*ruh-ruh-ruh-ruh-roo*—and Cleo's voice rang out a second after. "Max! Bedroom!"

The barking trailed off. After a few seconds of silence, the chain rattled in the lock. The door opened, and Cleo's round face peered out.

Those *eyes.* The sight of them hit Sylvie, whooshing out all her carefully held air, her professional-symmetrical smile. They really were purple, a ring of deep amethyst fading to hazel flecks around the pupil.

"Nina," Sylvie called across the office. "*Nina.*" She balled up a takeout napkin, hesitated, tossed it at her friend. Her work friend. Nina flinched and popped out her earbuds.

"Jesus, what?"

"Get over here." She already had the full photo spread pulled up. When Nina appeared behind her chair, Sylvie watched her eyes go huge in the computer screen reflection and felt the shimmery glow of satisfaction.

"No way those aren't fake."

Sylvie popped up a new window with the results from all the apps—untouch.me, faceVirgin, TRUU—over a picture of sweet baby Cleo holding up a caught fish next to her grinning face. Apart from a few minor and completely understandable edits on her recent posts, Cleo was 100% natural. "She's just a little self-conscious about her jawline, that's all. You really think I wouldn't check first?"

"Oh my God." Nina leaned forward onto the desk and unpinched her fingers over Sylvie's screen, zooming in on Cleo's purple eyes until they dissembled into pixels. "Ugh, can you imagine one of the baby Hadids with these? *Starstruck*. How'd you find her?"

Scrolling through insta and Facebook and the quasi-legal Panopti.com late at night, curling into a smaller and smaller ball under her blankets, thinking *please please please*, thinking *why are you posting fake shit*, thinking of the meeting where Jay had laid his hand on the back of her chair and she'd frozen, little rabbit. Dumb little pet-store bunny, looking up and expecting a smile. Getting his tight look of disapproval instead. "You're not a new hire anymore. You don't have any more excuses." Sylvie swallowed, opened her email, started composing. "I just give the universe good vibes, and she rewards me."

"Gross. Woo-woo." Nina straightened up. As she headed back to her desk, she threw over her shoulder, "Enjoy the commission, hon."

Sylvie paused in the middle of typing her introduction ("I'm a donor consultant for Beau&Bio, the genetic choice and therapy firm—"). Always the commission. She copied Jay on the email before she sent it, trying not to glance at his glass-walled office. As if the commission was why she worked her ass off. She swept her fingers across the screen, minimizing the email, the app results, returning her photo spread to its proper size. Toddler Cleo in overalls, her dense little eyebrows furrowed. Little Cleo in a Santa hat, hugging a black and white pitbull mix and laughing up at the camera. Teenage Cleo, her dark hair resting against the silvery temple of a sleeping old woman. Cleo speaking at a lectern with a huge northwest Native design projected on the wooden wall behind her. (Was it Quileute? Tillamook? Sylvie knew researching would be respectful.

She just hadn't found time yet.) Cleo in a red bodycon dress and feathery eyelashes, blowing a kiss and winking; Cleo in a cap and gown, holding a diploma above her head with her parents alongside her. And, in one of the most recent pictures: Cleo in the golden light of a school gym, swooping across the floor in one of those long powwow dresses and a black shawl, trailing rainbow streamers behind her like wings. In every photo, Cleo's eyes shone, purple stars tracing a constellation across the collage that looked like luck, that looked like a new life.

A thumbs-up emoji from Jay popped up in the work chat, its cheerful *ding* mismatched with Sylvie's nosediving mood. A thumbs up? That was it? Before she could stop herself, she peeked at his office. Something fluttered inside her. Jay was grinning at her—only at her—across the open floorplan, his chiseled jawline elevating the expression to something angelic. Some people said he'd gotten his look off a derelict Texan rancher, only divining the guy's handsomeness from old yearbook photos. His first big break as a donor consultant. Nina disagreed, swore the jaw was from the Uruguayan taxi driver for the 2039 holiday collection. Sylvie couldn't care less about where the genes had originated. He'd made them his own.

She touched her fingertips to her overheated cheeks, stared back at Cleo's photos. Yes. There was no way that Cleo's eyes couldn't mean a new, better, lovelier life. A lovelier life for both of them.

And here they were, about to start living it.

"Hi! Hi. I'm Sylvie Nikos." Sylvie's arm shot out, fingers tingling at the prospect of first contact. Her charm bracelets tinkled, then shrank into silence as Cleo looked at the waiting hand.

"Cleo Lester." She took Sylvie's hand in a loose grip and let go quickly. "I was making coffee, do you want some?"

Not "Can I offer you a drink?", not "What would you like?". Oh, but that was ungrateful, Sylvie thought, catching herself. "That would be lovely, thank you," she said.

Cleo vanished from the door, and Sylvie squeezed inside, her nose wrinkling immediately at the musty scent.

"You can put your galoshes in the box," Cleo called from the kitchen. Sylvie spotted the plastic bin already brimming with overshoes and rainboots, including a yellow pair with turquoise fish and a glittery, Chelsea-style set. Cute.

She set her overshoes in the box, trying not to touch the goop on the soles. "I love your—"

That was as far as she got before the dog started barking again, the noise barely muffled by the closed door. "Max! Sit!"

A couple soft *woofs,* and then Max quieted. "Good boy, Max," Cleo said. Sylvie heard the sound of a dog clicker as she emerged into the living/dining/kitchen area. She headed for the green sofa that slouched next to the balcony's sliding glass door, but Cleo set down two coffee mugs with definitive clunks on the dining table. Sylvie changed course.

She was already staring around the apartment as she slid into the worn wooden chair. Cleo had her back turned in the kitchen as she snagged something from the fridge, so Sylvie had a couple moments to enjoy herself. It was one of her favorite parts of the job, looking around like, "Would I expect someone with *those* cheekbones to live here?" or "With the money they'll get from *that* nose, what could this place look like?" For Cleo, Sylvie had imagined a little cottage—that was the word she used, even though she knew the alt-text on her mental picture would read "shack"—with a few black chickens scratching the soil and, for some reason, a spindly red windmill.

Instead, it was just a cute little apartment around the size of the first one Sylvie had gotten after college. Cleo was a year older than her—but everyone got there in their own time. Out on the matchbox balcony, a couple of jungle-like geraniums spilled out of their plastic pots in cascades of green and pink. A novelty lamp shaped like a T. rex sat on the glass end table next to the (thrifted? Dumpster dived?) couch. There was a book there, a beat-up paperback, but Sylvie couldn't tell what it was.

Cleo's clothes were kind of raggedy too, a pink UW sweatshirt with "Class of 2036" written on it in peeling letters and a pair of ratty brown teddy bear slippers. Usually people dressed up for these meetings. Sylvie certainly had. Though perhaps it was just a question of what she could afford, since even Cleo's TV had that curved sleekness that had gone out of style sometime in the early 30s. Honestly, the only things in the place that looked really "new" were the squishy fleece dog bed and Cleo herself. That long, shiny dark hair, the way she carried herself. She had really great skin age, too, despite the tween-esque zit healing on her chin.

Sylvie bit down on her recommendation for her favorite anti-microbial green tea cream as Cleo brought over a tray with a sugar bowl, a cream carton, and a drip-style coffee pot. Cleo sank into the seat across from her, poured for herself first.

"So." She fixed those startling eyes on Sylvie.

"So!" Sylvie added cream and two spoonfuls of sugar. Cleo's purple gaze followed the teaspoon as it dipped into the sugar bowl and rose again. Whatever. She'd never been able to stomach black coffee. "How're things?"

Cleo's eyes narrowed for a half-second, just long enough that Sylvie wasn't sure if it had been just a blink. Outside, the sound of a car whooshing through water, the hard splatter of tidal flood on the sidewalks. "Things are great," she gushed. "I mean, it's been *so* long since we've had a chance to catch up."

She tilted her head and grinned, a perfect SilVal college girl made good.

Oh, Sylvie realized, so she was one of *those* donors.

Well, that shouldn't be an issue. At the retreat last year, her first with the company, Jay had given this great talk in the morning circle. Sylvie had paid some attention, but mostly she was just loving the first rays of sun sparkling on El Capitan. She caught sight of two fire-colored songbirds chasing and looping each other among the trees, and Jay's voice wove among their wings: Every interaction a dance, every donor the lead. They chose when to open the door, to shake her hand, to offer her a drink. All she had to do was swing at their fingertips and wait for the bow and curtsy.

So Sylvie laughed. "That's a good voice! Have you done any acting?"

Cleo rapped her nails against her mug. "No."

In the silence, Sylvie heard Max sniffing at the bottom of the bedroom door. Cleo stared at Sylvie, looking like she'd been carved from hardwood. Oh, but was that a bad thought? A stereotype of Native people? An impulse seized her: Grab her bag, throw the contract on the table, pin the arm and draw the blood. But that's not how things were done.

Not really, anyway.

"Have you heard anything from that purple-eyed girl?" Jay asked from across the meeting room.

Sylvie closed her laptop. "Um, no. But it's only been five days. Isn't that too early for a follow-up?"

Jay toggled the display switch on the conference table, and the summer lineup crystallized on the cherrywood as though midstride on a catwalk. A half-dozen holograms with the best sequences Beau&Bio had to offer sashayed in place, their legs forming a shifting, ghostly fence between Sylvie and her boss. A pair of translucent ginger-freckled calves slid back and forth in front of Jay's face, twisting the flat line of his mouth into a grimace, warping that perfect jaw. "We're starting pre-orders *next week*. No, it is not too early for a follow-up."

"I'm sorry. I'll send one now." She reopened her laptop, hesitated over the screen. Ugh, she was going to seem so pushy. Not a good dance partner at all.

"Great." Jay was already back on his phone.

Sylvie bit her tongue. Maybe *he* shouldn't have already sent a finalized roster to his boss Artie, who'd passed it on, blissfully stupid, to marketing. Maybe it wasn't fair that Sylvie, the littlest and lowest, was being asked to do the most. Maybe, if this kind of work was a dance, then Jay should hold her close and steady when he dipped her. She blinked. Her eyes stung.

Next to her, Nina's ringed hands flew over her keyboard, her gaze glued to whatever she was working on. The new guy, Aidan, slid her the box of bagels that was going around. Sylvie passed it on, ignoring the twist in her stomach. "Sorry, I'm a donut girl."

The last hologram's lilac eyes glittered—the artists had even given her a little bit of a smize. There they were, so close. Sylvie set her jaw and opened a new email. Cleo was probably busy. She just needed a follow-up, a reminder. A reminder to not be a life-ruining bitch.

Eight days. Eight days and ten follow-ups and two hundred fifty-seven preorders, until Jay came clean to Artie, and Artie authorized an extra financial incentive for the purple-eyed girl. Sylvie undid the clasp on her bag slower than she usually would have, letting herself pet the creamy leather exterior. She'd bought it with the cash from her first commission (a teen boy with gem-sharp cheekbones—he said he'd use the money for college). Clearing her throat, Sylvie set the folder on the table between them. Inside were the promises: fifty milliliters of blood for fifty thousand dollars, and a transferral of gene sequence ownership and rights to Beau&Bio for an additional twenty-five thousand. Already signed, although the donor could back out right up until Sylvie took the blood. Consent laws. Sylvie smiled again at Cleo, trying to make the expression reach her eyes.

"Well, I wanted to say thank you for meeting with me on such short notice. We don't usually approach people in the wild so soon, so . . . ." She blew the steam off her coffee, took a sip. It was still too bitter—the aftertaste was like burnt earth on her tongue. She probably shouldn't have said "in the wild."

"In the wild, huh? So I'm pretty special." Cleo flipped open the file, looked at the photo of her eyes paper-clipped to the first page.

"All of our donors are special." She said the words so often that they rose out of her throat automatically, but it was true. Every single person she'd ever visited was unique in a way that *meant* something, even if other people wore their gene sequences better. Cleo needed to know that. "I mean, it's not just about how someone's hair is so curly, or how long their legs are. It's about the way their curls bounce when they laugh, or the way they fold up their legs under their skirt when they sit down."

The way they fit in with their furniture and decor and dirty dishes, their natural light and bedtime routine and city skyline. Sylvie could see a thousand v-stream kittens and a million glossy models with that hair, those legs, but she would never forget how they looked on their first owner. She owed them that, at the very least. "I mean, you're *people.* You're *you.*"

Cleo's eyes had gone stony. "Wow, that's so generous of you."

"Um." Wait, no, dammit. Sylvie shifted in her chair. "I'm sorry, I feel like I've offended you?"

Cleo leaned back, the soft edges of her round face vanishing into anger. "How could you offend me?"

"Um, maybe some of my wording was wrong?" She picked up the coffee pot and refilled Cleo's mug. She was just trying to do her goddamn job. "I'm so sorry, I didn't mean it like that."

"Oh, well, how *did* you mean it?"

Cleo wrapped her hands tight around her coffee mug. Sylvie couldn't look at her face anymore, just at the girl's knuckles going paler and paler, the bitten fingernails hard hard against the ceramic. She shrugged, then tried to speak, and then Cleo said, "Because I mean, I've already signed all your paperwork, right? So why can't you just send me to one of your clinics and take my blood there? Why do you have to come into my *home*?"

Max whined, but Cleo didn't quiet him this time. Sylvie could feel those purple eyes staring her down. The hologram model with the amethyst eyes, dissolving into mist. Jay's growing agitation, the sound of his quick stride crossing the floor to her desk after his meeting with Artie, the hand biting down on her shoulder and the whisper hissed in her ear. *Fuck this up and you're done here.* Nina pretending not to hear. The preorders flooding in, setting a first-day record, Aidan touching her arm to congratulate her and Sylvie shrinking away. The champagne in the office, bubbles hitting her nose, Jay grim in the corner. The dance between donor and consultant, between worker and boss. The stomach-drop feeling of falling towards the floor.

Why was she in Cleo's home. Even though Sylvie's whole body had that tingly, I'm-in-trouble stillness, even though her eyes were hot and stinging, she remembered what to say. Emphasize the care, not the possibility of donor poaching. "Beau&Bio's consultants pride themselves on being with their donors for every step of the donation process."

Cleo snorted. "And what about after that, huh? I notice you don't do royalties. How much money is your company making off of me? How much money are *you* making off of me?"

"I don't make that much money!" Tears splashed down her face and onto the table. Traces of eye glitter swam in the drops like gold dust. Across the table, Cleo's lip curled. The training videos said to keep your tone cheerful, compassionate, like doing both was so easy with a donor like Cleo. Sylvie sniffled, bounced her voice up an octave. "I'm trying to help you."

"Right, because people like you love helping people like me." Cleo spat. She crossed her arms tight over her sweatshirt as though hiding her veins. "You're a fucking parasite."

People like you. Oh, so Sylvie was a racist. Sylvie was a *bad person.* Sylvie didn't see donors as people. Sylvie brought her cheap plastic overshoes to splash in sea-sewage puddles outside Cleo's rundown apartment for funsies.

She surged to her feet, sending the chair clattering back onto the linoleum. The dog went crazy in the bedroom. Standing over Cleo, she felt electric, huge, a beautiful billboard person this trash could never even hope to be. "I took this job to help people. I took this job to find beauty, and to pay people for that beauty, and to show that beauty to everyone." She swept her arm out, charm bracelets ringing. "And if that makes me a fucking parasite, then you're the *person* who volunteered to take my money."

No response, except for the dog. Cleo's chair squeaked across the floor as she stood up and met Sylvie's eyes with her own steady, furious gaze. They were the same height, Sylvie realized. She swallowed. Cleo looked down, gathered up the mugs and the coffeepot. Each made a fragile *clink* on the glass tray. Sylvie stared at the pale part in Cleo's shiny hair, then at the waving tip of her braid as she strode to the kitchen counter. The dog was still barking, high-pitched, panicked.

"Sit, Max!" Cleo called, and Sylvie flinched. Max whined, scratched at the door.

Clattering dishes in the sink, hissing water from the faucet. Everyday noise, the soundtrack of mornings in Sylvie's empty apartment. Another car passed.

Awareness flooded back into Sylvie's fingers. Her hands were shaking. The chair lay overturned behind her, incongruous as a dream image. Had she—? The memory of her lips moving superimposed over her now slack mouth: *you're the person who volunteered to take my money.* The water shut off, and the shaking spread up through Sylvie's arms, down towards her hips, her knees. She managed to set the chair upright and sank into it, staring at the water-stained tabletop.

"Max! Lie down!" Now there was silence. Cleo probably expected her to leave. Sylvie kept staring down at the wood grain. If she left now, grabbed her overshoes and stood on the flooded sidewalk, then . . . something yawned open in her stomach and beneath her feet. She felt like that untethered astronaut grabbing for the ISS door. There'd been a video of it happening, years ago, the astronaut's face invisible in their mirrored helmet. Their thick white gloves grasping, again and again. Catching only void. Half the comments beneath just read, *god i wish that were me.* Sylvie mouthed it. Under her thoughts, under the sound of the rain pouring down on the tiled balcony and the overgrown geraniums, she heard the *clik-clek* of the dog clicker again. "Good boy, Max."

Then, Cleo's purple gaze pressed down on her. "You. Take the blood and get out."

"What?" She startled up, staring at Cleo.

Cleo's mouth twisted. She sat in the chair next to Sylvie and pushed up her sweatshirt sleeve. "Just take it, okay?"

Sylvie stared, then fumbled for her gear, laid the Beau&Bio Venipuncture Kit out on the table. Oh my God, it was happening. The interior of Cleo's arm was a lighter shade of brown than the rest of her skin, the vein a barely-visible green river. The words of the script switched on in her brain. "Make a fist, please." Sylvie sanitized her hands, willing them to stop shaking, willing her breath to calm as the alcohol scent stung her nostrils. Blue gloves on. Cleo's vein swabbed, shiny amber with iodine. Multisample needle broken out of crinkly packaging, positioned at the palpated vein, silver tip star-bright. "You may want to look away."

Cleo didn't. Sylvie pushed into the vein. Cleo let out a long breath through her nostrils, and Sylvie glanced up at her as she attached the first sample tube, hoping Cleo's purple eyes would meet hers, hoping that if she was crying, it was with relief. Seventy-five thousand dollars—the things someone like Cleo could do with that money. "What will you buy?" Sylvie asked. Cleo said nothing, but that was okay. That was okay now.

As Sylvie watched the deep red blood pulse into the sample tube, her own breathing calmed. She always got this sense of fullness from watching the collection process, a kind of sleepy buzz. She disengaged the warm sample tube, snapped on the cap that contained the anticoagulant, shook it, attached the next tube. Whatever type of dancing Cleo did, it had made her strong. Her muscles were tense under Sylvie's hand. "I saw the photo of you dancing, you know. With the shawl?"

Cleo stiffened.

"You looked so graceful," Sylvie said. The second tube was about half-full. "It must take so much hard work."

Out of the corner of her eye, Sylvie saw Cleo's hand twitch towards the needle. The procedure was a little uncomfortable, Sylvie knew. "I'm sorry that there isn't an easier way to do this." But she'd take care of Cleo. She cared. "And I'm sorry that I yelled earlier. That was mean."

"It's whatever." Cleo said.

A response. Progress. Sylvie cleared her throat, detached the second tube. When she shook it, the blood frothed into bubbles like red seafoam. Cleo's eyes fixed on it, still avoiding her. Sylvie wanted to reach out and take her hand. Instead, she removed the needle and held a cotton ball over the puncture point.

"You know, I'd love to meet Max before I go," Sylvie said. Cleo batted her fingers away and pressed down on the cotton. "He seems like a really sweet dog."

Cleo finally looked at Sylvie. Whenever Sylvie spotted the billboards, the insta ads, the models—she'd see Cleo's eyes now, in this moment, forever. Maybe Sylvie would do what Jay did. Maybe she'd spend her commission on getting her first therapy, so that whenever she glanced in the mirror, she'd remind herself that she had made these amethyst eyes her own, that she'd made this new life belong to her.

But—Cleo's gaze wasn't grateful. Sylvie watched, confused, as Cleo took a deep breath. Pinned her with those purple eyes.

"Get out of my house."

Back when you could lease basement apartments in this part of town, Cleo's grandmother had one, rent-controlled and therefore priceless. Her grandmother had kept the place for years, watched the neighbors go from red-eyed working moms to artistic types who were too clean-cut to actually be artists. She had peered out beyond the chain lock with narrowed eyes while young WASPy couples flitted around the movers like invasive songbirds. She stood guard until Cleo, there for a sleepover, whined for mac and cheese.

Over the years, the neighbors vanished, all of them replaced by a single newcomer: the sea. Bubbling out of the toilet, dripping through the window, washing over the floor. The last time she visited with her parents, Cleo's mom had opened the door and a little wave dashed out and soaked Cleo's socks. The fancy shawl Cleo worked on side-by-side with her grandmother still hung on the wall, its ribbons wavered on the water's surface like kelp fronds. Cleo waited on the stairs during the argument—*you can't stay here, Mom, it's a shithole*—and helped carry Gramma's things to their sedan once it ended.

Whenever she danced in that shawl afterwards, the ribbons seemed a little heavier at the ends. Stiff with salt.

Cleo stood by the balcony window and watched a beat-to-shit Escalade slosh to a stop outside. The Beau&Bio girl ran to it, shielding her sleek hair. The second her silver loafer disappeared inside, Cleo's shoulders dropped, and she pressed a hand to the aching interior of her elbow. For a moment, the only things that moved were the round geranium leaves bouncing in the downpour and the crystal raindrops sliding down the glass. Should she make mac and cheese? With honey mustard and breakfast sausages, the kind Gramma made? No. It didn't feel right. She crossed the room, dropped the mug the Beau&Bio girl had drunk from in the trash can. That didn't feel right either. She picked up the mug and scrubbed it at the sink until her fingers reddened and the sponge squeaked against the ceramic. She imagined every trace of the girl—her dark lipstick smudges, her whirled fingerprints, her microdroplets of saliva—swirling down the drain. The double helix of her DNA disappearing into that dark void. She set the clean mug to the side. There. That felt right.

She didn't own this apartment. Her parents rented too. What places did they have between them where they could set their feet and refuse to budge? These hands, these legs. Sometimes she caught herself in the middle of frying eggs or practicing dance or making endless phone calls and thought *this is mine.* She fell in love with her fingertips the way some people loved the squeak of their front doors.

In the other room, Max whimpered. "It's okay, baby, it's okay," she singsonged. She let herself into the bedroom, closed the door behind her as Max sniffed at her ankles and hands with his chilly pink and black nose. "Good boy, Max." She petted him—one brown ear, one white ear—until his eyes half-closed in happiness.

Outside her narrow window, the rain was coming down harder than ever, sounding like one long, staticky yell. Cleo wanted to tuck herself into her unmade bed, hug the heavy blankets up around her eyes, let Max rest at her feet (for once not reminding him that he had his own bed). But the tide was already changing, flowing back out into Puget Sound. Max needed to go for a walk, and she needed to visit her grandmother.

Max grumbled when she pulled the doggy raincoat over his head, but at the bus, he wagged his stumpy tail when he saw Jim was driving. Jim passed Cleo a milk-bone as she boarded, asked how she was doing. Cleo stared for a moment. *I just sold my genes for more money than I make in a year.* "Oh, you know," she said. Max snuffled at her hand for the treat.

By the time they disembarked, the sidewalk was wet with rain but free of sea-sewage, Max's claws tapping against the concrete instead of splashing, then crunching as they turned onto Emerald Memorial's gravel paths. Though it was the weekend, Cleo could hear the heavy whirr and grind of the excavator crews in the cemetery. People didn't like the idea of their loved ones drowning, even if they were already dead, and the city didn't like the idea of someone stepping out of their restored Craftsman to find a washed-up coffin. It was just a matter of time.

Around the columbarium wall, the cherry trees drooped, their blossoms soaked with the recent downpour. Cleo inhaled. The air was sweet here, the everpresent scent of salt an afterthought. At her grandmother's niche, she found a few pink petals stuck to the marble and picked them off (saying a firm "*No*" to Max when he tried to eat them) before pressing the hologram's power button.

Gramma shivered into the air, her permed black hair tossed back over one shoulder, her mouth frozen in a playful grin. Even with the discount her dad's friend had offered, they'd only been able to afford this still image, lifted from a photo taken during her honeymoon. Her yellow skirt, whirling around her calves, flickered as the rain disturbed its light. Cleo sat back on the bench, her raincoat rustling beneath her, and stared up at her grandmother. At her purple eyes that were so vivid, even in this semi-translucent state.

Seventy-five thousand dollars. Maybe she'd buy a place on Whidbey Island now that all the rich white retirees were fleeing their vacation homes. She'd grab one of the little bungalows dirt-cheap from a pair of desperate Gen X-ers. They'd be trying to avoid reentering the job market as their nest egg trickled away into the Pacific, and she'd be reclaiming Snohomish land, or, at least, she would be when it was land again. She could only have it once they were done, once they didn't want it anymore.

But would they ever sell it so cheap, even just the down payment? And how would she afford any of the installments after that? And when her parents needed help with medical bills, would she just say "Sorry, I can't?" And when her debts came due, would she watch her accounts fall to zero? And when she looked in the mirror tomorrow morning, would she still have her grandmother's eyes, or would they belong to someone else?

These eyes, these hands, these legs. A few cherry blossoms, lifted by the wind, soared through her grandmother's form, distorting her for a moment. In her college courses, Cleo had read the testimonies from over a century ago, the ones about the salmon run: They said that the waves used to be more fish than water; that the twisting silver-green bodies rose and crashed in the breakers; that the air was thick with birds.

She'd check the real estate listings in the morning. She'd work and she'd wait, and she'd buy when she could afford it. When the time was right, she'd put her grandmother's picture on the mantel, wrapped in plastic to keep her safe from the rising waters, the rising waters that would fill the home and warp its wooden floors, that would flow up the walls until the plaster swelled and cracked, that would lap at the ceiling in light-filled ripples and glow at night with bioluminescent creatures—shifting, swirling, spiraling in the tides. They'd stay like that for years, crabs settling like kittens on the rotting armchairs, anemones sprouting like memorial flowers on the photo frames. Years and years, and the sun and the air and the wildflower earth just a dream floating somewhere in the attic.

And when it was all over, eighty years or a century from now, when it was all over and the waves had sunk back into the ocean, her grandchildren would stand on their land and watch the sun come out over the mountains, over the unsunken city. Those first rays would hit. The dirt would sparkle with salt crystals. The earth and the air and the house would smell like salt. And what would grow? Salt.

But only at first, and not forever.

Bernie Jean Schiebeling (she/they) is calling on you to join the struggle for liberation by Palestinian, Indigenous, and oppressed peoples everywhere. Set aside the individual catharsis of short-term activism: embrace community, embrace longevity, embrace the possibility and inevitability of change. Stand together to fight the demands of empire. Rest together, and help the garden grow more than salt.

A Move to a New Country

Dan Musgrave

The 𐓏𐓘𐓻𐓘𐓻𐓟[1] were a sky people first before we came down to the Earth to begin a new life. One dawn, a week before 𐒻𐓲𐓣[2] went into the hospital, we faced east and watched a pillar of white smoke reach up into the stratosphere. The rocket was carrying some of us up to become sky people again. If 𐒻𐓲𐓣 had her way, she would be standing right here in two months watching me make the same trip.

"Woo Woo Woo! Go!" she hollered, as if the rocket needed encouragement. One hand clapped her thigh while the other kept her coffee mug at the ready. The dry foliage in the yard trembled in the roar of the rocket's launch. 𐒻𐓲𐓣 coughed a few times from all the excitement, but didn't spill a drop of coffee. "Look at that little thing go, grandson."

"It's three times as tall as the house," I said.

"Not to me it ain't."

A small fire burned in a rusted fire pit at our feet. She judged the growing light, then reached back to set her coffee down and grab a few sprigs of cedar from the baggie on her lawn chair.

"I'm gonna send up a message to your momma," she said. A sliver of sun crested the horizon. "Right up there in Cassiopeia with all the rest of the women who commit the sin of knowing their own worth."

She tossed the cedar into the humble flame, took the new smoke into her cupped hands and bathed in it. Reached to the sky, welcomed the sun. Once, twice. Four times in total.

I joined in. Mom, I composed in my head, please help. Either convince 𐒻𐓲𐓣 to go or give me the guts to stay.

We stood in silence for a while, smoke from our small fire chasing the rocket's tail. Eventually, 𐒻𐓲𐓣 shuffled inside. I stayed, mulling talking points to try on her and abandoning them each in turn. Trying not to imagine what I would do with myself if I stayed.

---

1. WaZhaZhe
2. Iko

How we would survive in a world that was dying.

When I came in, 𐒻𐒽𐓂 was settled in her recliner, coffee mug refilled and steaming, watching a stream of an old tennis match.

The savor of bacon filled the house, all fat and salt and grease. My mouth watered. On the screen, some poor, unranked guy from Western Europe was serving to Rafa Nadal, her all-time favorite. It was old—older than me, even. Something she'd seen live as a kid. She'd seen this match a hundred times already—probably—but everytime I put on something current, she changed the channel. Said they'd ruined the sport with the smart rackets and smart balls and the lift of the body-mod ban. She most liked watching two young, fit, tan men, built from their own effort, panting and sweating. She most liked the past.

"𐒹𐒰𐓏𐒷[3], 𐒻𐒽𐓂," I greeted her as if I'd just come home.

"Bacon on the counter for you," she said. She lifted her chin and nodded back behind her at the kitchen, eyes glued to the match. A small cough escaped after another sip from the mug. On screen, Rafa fielded the serve and whipped it right back with such vicious English there was no way for no-name to return it. "Toast too, but I'm not gonna butter it for you, spaceman."

I went and grabbed a plate.

"𐒻𐒽𐓂, I know you don't want to talk about it, but we have to," I said through the kitchen pass-through. I loaded my plate, knowing to savor the gift of both her cooking and the bacon. "I have to tell them if we're going or staying."

"What's there to talk about? You're going. I'm not. 'S all there is to it." This said without emotion. Like it was no big deal. I looked down into my plate.

Everything was getting too dry. Too hot. The pinch was coming and every day now the rockets were delivering supplies and crew to the generation ship in low orbit. Passengers, human and not, were next. There was no 'later' left anymore, all we had was 'soon.' She knew it as well as I did.

Another serve from no-name. Rafa flipped it right back, moving his opponent to the left.

"𐓏𐒻𐓊𐓂𐓇𐒼𐒰[4], come. Sit. Don't think too hard, you'll pull

3. Ha.weh

4. wee-TSOH-shkah

something. Watch the match with me before you go to work. You'll never see a more wicked forehand."

The no-name volleyed, but his sneakers skidded a little too far in the red clay. A matter of inches, though that was enough. It was all over his face that he knew what would happen as soon as he made contact.

I pulled a chair from the coffee table and sat next to the recliner, plate in my lap. "𐒻𐒽𐓂, I can't go if you don't."

"Bullcocky," she said. "You go to work every day without me. It's the same as that, just slightly longer."

On the TV, Rafa fielded the volley, barely breathing hard, and zinged it down the sideline, right at the deadman's corner at the baseline.

"Please. The 𐓷𐓘𐓻𐓘𐓻𐓟 are making a move to a new country. It's time to go."

"Grandson." She turned to face me. "You're full of knowledge, maybe even more than me. But I know when you're talking about something you got from a book."

The last time we'd made a move to a new country was before 𐒻𐒽𐓂 was born, when we were forced from Kansas down onto a reservation in Oklahoma. Of course I'd had to read about it in a book.

"𐒻𐒽𐓂, the Council declared it."

Rafa's opponent raced to catch the ball, but he couldn't recover fast enough from the skid. He stretched out, flailing mostly.

"Those old coots declare lots of things. S'what they do. Whole point of running for office is so they can go shaking hands, declaring this and that up and down the road all day."

I looked at the plate in my lap. Her blue-ringed irises were too mirthful, given the topic. I couldn't meet them. It felt like I was already leaving her. Or maybe that she was leaving me. It was the same either way.

"You're a good boy," she said, patting my hand and turning back to the TV. "That's why you get some of the last of my bacon. So, eat up. You're too skinny. You'll need your strength for the launch."

The neon green ball bounded to a halt. Game, set, match. No-name already had his face buried in a towel.

I pulled the folded infographic from my pocket and put it on the end table next to her seat. Then I piled all my strips of bacon onto my toast, folded it in half, and took a bite, returning my plate to the sink.

"I love you," I said, planting a greasy kiss on top of her head.

"I know." She smiled and sipped from her coffee. "Now go tell them 𐓲𐓟[5] who's boss."

At work, I had to focus primarily on the buffalo, which were an entirely different kind of problem. Or a component of the bigger problem. We could get them on the ship and into their pens, that was easy. Well, it was easy considering it was like trying to push a temperamental car into a too-small parking spot and a wrong move could get you gored or trampled. There were so many ranch hands and cowboys among us, though, we could usually move them around just fine. We could sedate them and secure them in modified crash cushioning to keep them contained for their launch. We knew they could handle the *g*'s; even monkeys and dogs could do that. That's how the space program started. The trouble was that for every buffalo who came, we had to leave someone behind.

The spreadsheet in front of me was an inventory of life. Noah's shopping list, basically. The grasses—indiangrass, big bluestem, little bluestem, and switchgrass—were all collected and planted already. The sacred medicines too—sweetgrass, tobacco, cedar, sage, and 𐓨𐓘𐓤𐓘 𐓸𐓪𐓬𐓟[6]. But the buffalo, deer, Virginia opossum, three species of bats, jackrabbits, raccoons, pocket gophers and their cousins, some dozens of mice species, and the rest of the mammals were harder. Not to mention the reptiles, amphibians, and birds. And the insects—many of which had already gone extinct in the last couple decades—we were having to be creative with, even importing some of our cricket stock from breeders. Every entry I made there was another human name left off the passenger manifest. The floor trembled as another rocket took off from the launch complex further out in the prairie.

---

5. Tse
6. Mahn-KAH XOH-beh

"There's just no good goddamn reason to take full-grown adults," Nik said. "It's a waste."

Nik was Lenape/Pawnee, not 𐓏𐒰𐓓𐒰𐓓𐒷, and he was sourer than an unripe cranberry most of the time and only getting worse with each passing day. But then he did husbandry, not research, so sourness was often useful. He had a place reserved for him and his family as payment for his work, but only them.

"You know the adults can handle the strain best," Jess said. Her beaded earrings didn't even sway as she said it. A veterinarian, even-keeled, she had lots of experience staying calm in the face of testy beasts. "This isn't arbitrary, it's scientific fact. And more importantly, the 𐓊𐒷 need their elders too."

"Oh, don't get me started on that," Nik scoffed. "Just tradish bullshit."

Something had changed. Nik was practical, efficient, and rangy, like he was made of jerky. He was an oxford-shirt-tucked-into-Wranglers kind of guy. He knew the logistics of herd management, the storing of feed and all those things that kept thousands of animals alive. He knew the business of ranching to the same degree that I knew how to balance closed ecological systems. I hadn't seen him so outwardly ruffled before.

"No—" Jess began.

"Yes." Nik stabbed her direction with an index finger. "We're not making some kind of statement. We need to save ourselves, not score Native points. This is about survival."

"Exactly. That's when we need our ways the most." Jess raised her voice a tick. It wasn't quite a shout, but it was as close as I ever heard her get to it. "Giving up all we are in the process? That's not surviving, it's just staying alive."

"But staying alive is pretty goddamn important, ennit? Kinda the bare minimum. You wanna be the one to tell my eight-year-old niece we chose a cow over her?"

"The only reason we're still here,"—Jess pointed out the window at Oklahoma, at what used to be called Indian Territory—"is we didn't lose ourselves."

"Hey," I said. They both turned to me like they hadn't noticed I was there. "We've already gone over all this. We've done the work and run the numbers. It's too late to change the plan."

"We're changing it every time the Okies hit us." Nik rubbed

his chin. "Until we lift off, it's in flux. We can still do the right thing."

"Nik—" I said, but he was already in motion. He scooped up his sweat-stained Dekalb hat from the desk and left.

I looked to Jess. "What was that all about?"

"His wife's family," she said. "They got denied. No appeals. Now she's not sure she can leave them."

"Oh. Just parents?"

"Got two sisters, too. Both married with kids. They were all trying to get in."

Outside, the rumble of another launch was punctuated by the small cracks of distant gunfire. Both becoming so common I hardly noticed them any more. Everywhere, all around us, everything was combusting.

I got the call from my neighbors that ᏁᏦᎤ had collapsed and gone to the hospital just as I was leaving. She had been out in her garden in the afternoon, probably humming to her plants trying to keep them strong in the intense heat, and started coughing. She didn't stop until she fell. The neighbors had to call 911 because I wasn't there for her.

I rushed to the tribal hospital. The yellow ball of the sun was fighting to get through the restless, red clouds of Oklahoma dirt being thrown into the atmosphere. White smoke rose from the fires sweeping through the ranchlands in the distance. I counted the mounds on the hilltop, black silhouettes silent against the sunset. There were eight. Eight more buffalo lost today.

She was lazing in her hospital bed, plastic cup of grape juice in hand, when I got there. Some kind of crime drama played on the TV.

"What's eating you, ᏑᎤᏍᏢᏍ[7]?" She only glanced my way, taking a sip of juice.

"I'm sorry, I rushed over as soon as I heard," I said. "How are you?"

---

7. TSOH-shkah

"Oh fine. Just a little inconvenienced is all."

"I was worried about you."

"Well what for?"

"ᏧᏦᎤ, are you serious?"

"Oh, I just took a spill and now they want me to stick around so they can take pictures of my insides. Probably to use as teaching materials about the ideal female form."

I couldn't help but laugh. I hadn't known what to expect. I scooted a chair next to her and settled in. We watched the cops on the show rough up a few suspects.

"There are rumors they're going to move up the passenger launches," I said.

"Thought I was feeling more rumbling in my feet from all those little rockets."

I wanted to press her about our decision, but the weight of the day hit me all at once. I bowed my head, hands laced behind it. "Okies hit the herd again. Haven't gotten the details yet, just saw the bodies out in the grass. They didn't even try to take any of it this time. Just left them up on the hill to rot. They were just—just killing. Not even trying to feed their families or anything. Just killing to do it."

"They were doing it to hurt us," she said. "Nothing about survival to it, just plain old spite, ᏍᏧᏃᎤᏊᏈᏁ. Same as it's always been. Even if they weren't afraid of us shooting back they would still be trying to get us indirect like that."

We sat for a time. Let it all simmer and fade into the background.

"They're going to finalize the passenger list in one week," I said, making eye contact. Let it hang there between us.

"Is everything ready up there? That was quick. Good for us being ahead of schedule for once."

"The ship's been ready," I said. "Double checked. Triple checked. Collecting all the plants and animals and getting them up there was the main thing. That and letting everyone say goodbye."

ᏧᏦᎤ shook her head. "Why didn't you just get married? It's not too late, actually. I bet if you got on them dating apps today you could find a partner before the deadline. Or just go out in the hallway and see which of the staff are available. Don't have to be perfect, but it's better than being alone, let me tell you. Got so much going for you, too. PhD, free ticket on a spaceship, good with animals. Whole package."

"ᏁᏦᏫ, please."

I waited for more snark, but she didn't continue. We knew what each other were thinking anyway. It didn't need to be released to be heard. Outside her window, night was coming down. She took my hand in hers and I leaned over and let my head rest awkwardly on her shoulder. She smelled like onions and earth.

"I can't go without you," I said. There was an emptiness in my stomach, where it seemed like I'd already left her behind by not being there when she fell, and all there was to me was just a hollowed-out-ness.

She let that sit. After a couple minutes, she pointed out the window at the night sky, darkness growing as the evening got deeper. "Remember when we used to stay up late and name as many as we could? Before your momma passed and went up there to join them. She'd say 'You can't keep that boy up so late,' but smiling, not real serious like, cause she liked that you were learning. Now she's looking down on us and probably even more thankful. Right around there."

"Up in Cassiopeia," I said. The wonky 'w' constellation was dimmer these days behind the atmospheric haze than it had been, but not unidentifiable.

"Yessir. Trapped up there for boasting about her beauty too much. Her and her daughter, Andromeda. It's a mean world to us women who have a habit of being a little too honest."

A steady wail of sirens went out and came back, like waves on the shore, dropping off new patients for the Clinic then heading out to get more. For what, we couldn't know. So many small emergencies occurring at all times amid the backdrop of the all-encompassing one nobody seemed to be rushing to help.

"She's up there," ᏁᏦᏫ whispered. "And I'll be up there with her soon enough."

"ᏁᏦᏫ—"

She patted my back.

"Shhh. We were sky people, isn't that what you keep telling me? Like I don't already know? I'm the one taught you that when we pass, we return to it. Flare up, passing the boundary between earth and sky like one of those rockets. We get turned into new stars up there to guide those we left behind. Thing about Cassiopeia is you can still see it from the Centauri system. Did you know that? Bet you didn't. It's true. She'll be with you always. Only from way out there, that angle, Earth and ᏫᏥᏃᏥᏦᎾ ᎻᏥ[8], old grandfather sun, will be part of it too."

I wanted to brush at my eyes, get any tears before they wet her hospital gown. I didn't want her to know I'd 'sprung a leak' as she would put it. But doing so would have given it away too, and so I stayed motionless, staring out the window at the night, leaning against my grandmother's steadiness.

The poachers kept coming back, harassing us every day, and that kept Nik busy so there'd been no more office arguments since the first. He had been called to try to change the herd's range away from the boundaries and split off the most valuable individuals to keep them safe for transport.

Ma was one of the chosen buffalo who'd already been moved inside a couple weeks ago. I was in a stall with her, the oldest cow we had, picking and combing brambles out of her hair, when he approached. Two kids at his side. Just one of them was his that I could recognize.

I focused on Ma. She was as close to a matriarch as the herd had, and for that she got a nice clean stall in the barn. Plus, she needed to be in top shape for the transfer to the ship. I escaped the office to come see her whenever the math of the move got to be too much. With ᏥᏦᎾ staying in the hospital, I was escaping here more often. Grooming and petting her, getting huffs and head shakes, the contented tremors that traveled down her flanks. She helped me remember why we were doing all of this.

At its peak, the herd was 2500 head. These days it was about a fifth of that. Drought, heat, and poaching had hit them the hardest. Ma had survived it all for nearly two decades. Sure, during the rutting season, one or two huge bulls were in charge. Different ones every few years, too, as some new challenger in his prime inevitably

8. wee-TSEE-goh meen

took over. But the rest of the year? That was Ma's time to rule. She huffed at Nik.

He put an arm on the top of the stall door, leaned his chin on his forearm, and gave Ma a scratch on the curls of her forehead. I kept on brushing, moving down her flank. "Nik. Herd okay?"

"Gettin' by," he said. "They're real pissy out there. The launches, the Okies. They're hungry and thirsty too. Really on edge. Like most everyone, I guess. You remember Lucy? This is her cousin Melanie. Say hi, girls."

"Hi," I said to them.

"I heard about your grandma," Nik said. "How is she?"

"Okay," I said. I wondered who he heard it from.

"Think her situation is going to impact your reservations?" he asked. Tried to be casual about it but he was working his jaw harder than a bull chewing frozen cud.

So that was what he wanted.

"Not yet," I said.

"Time's running out." Nik took his hat in his hands and worked at the bill, folding it mercilessly. "You ever consider just deciding yourself and then making her live with it?"

I set the brush down and patted Ma on the hind end. "Wouldn't do any good. She'd kick my ass first and then pull strings to get it fixed second. For her, it's only she stays and I go."

"Yeah, yeah." Nik nodded. "Be hard to abandon her though. Given the circumstances. That'd be hard, wouldn't it, Melanie? To leave your granny behind?"

"Uh huh," the child said.

"Yeah," Lucy agreed.

Nik looked out the barn door like he was trying to see all the way to Tulsa. The girls split away and looked into the other stalls. Nik didn't watch them go, just kept staring. "If you give us your spots I'll leave our land to you."

"Nik—" I started.

"Got 25 acres that aren't wasteland. Soil's not spent yet so we can grow a few things. Not like before, but some. House isn't in too bad shape, but the frack-quakes are taking a toll. Most importantly, got a good well. A deep one. Water's cleaner than the bottled stuff."

"Are you serious right now?" I shook my head, turned back to Ma and started brushing her all over again.

"You just think on it." He seated his hat back down on his head. "Girls," he called.

He put one hand on a shoulder of each of the girls. "You could be set up as much as anyone can be to make a go at it down here. And," he inclined his chin down at the children, "you'd be saving some lives."

I turned away from him. I didn't want him to read anything in my face.

The 𐒼𐒰𐒹𐒻𐒼𐒷[9] was on all the screens in the hospital that afternoon, making an announcement about the accelerated launch schedule.

"We've made a move to a new country before," he was saying on the broadcast. 𐒻𐒼𐓂 was sleeping, or at least pretending to, in the hospital bed beside me. "Ever since we came to this land, long time ago. Always changing, adapting, growing. We studied the stars in the sky; we knew they never moved backwards and we couldn't either. So we kept going, no matter what we faced. Few hundred years ago, when the US Government was moving in, pushing us out, we had to make several moves to a new country in a 50 year period. From East Missouri to West. Then to Kansas. When they wanted that, then we moved from Kansas to Indian Territory. To here."

"Can I come in?" A young doctor peeked around the curtain that gave us privacy from the hall. When she slid it back and joined us, I recognized her from the newsfeeds. One of the Hunka family. She was tall and used to be a bigshot volleyball player at OU. The kind of person that made the whole county proud. Didn't know she was back and a doctor to boot, though we'd never really run in the same circles. I liked being outside in the dirt, she liked being inside on the hardcourt. She went to practice, I went to the public library and read fantasy novels.

I tried to focus on the broadcast so it wouldn't seem like I was staring.

"We gave up our old ceremonies then," the speech continued. "They were for another place and another time. Needed a whole

9. gah-HEE-geh

new way of being. New dances. We changed what we did, but it didn't change who we were. We will be the same even after this. They sent us to this wild barren place they didn't want (until they did). This place that happened to be packed full of all that oil. And we sold it and they burned it and we made a lot of money, took care of our people. But we hurt our world. We were a part of that. We have that stain on our hands. So, we put those earnings into our future—"

"𐒹𐒰𐓏𐒷." Dr. Hunka planted herself on a rolling stool that was far too short for her, tablet in her hands. "So, I'm sure they've already told you it's the lungs," she said. She turned the tablet toward me so I could see the black and white images. I could see the ghost of ribs and the white network of what looked like spiderwebs. Like the charts of constellations. "Same thing we're all going to get if we stay here, basically. Not that that helps. Sorry."

She pointed at the ceiling in a circular motion with her stylus. "It's the air. All the dust and exhaust. Basically, it's the same as if every breath we took was from a cigarette now. Here, this is scarring and inflammation. Emphysema. She spend a lot of time outdoors still? Yeah, I figured. Bunch of elders do. If it was 20 years ago, or she was 20 years younger, they would put her on a waitlist for a donor at this stage. Nowadays.... Can I ask, is she on the passenger list?"

"We are," I rushed to say. On the TV, the 𐒼𐒰𐒹𐒻𐒼𐒷 was still going on about carrying our history with us into the future. Thanking everyone he could think of as he went. Talking about the need for community at times like this.

"That's your best bet at this point," she said. "There will be clean air on the ship. We can't heal the damage, but it can be managed with acceptable discomfort."

"Acceptable discomfort? What kind of nonsense is that? And why are you all talking like I'm not sitting right here?" 𐒻𐒼𐓂 sat like a little spark plug, arms crossed, bottom lip pushed out, one eyebrow raised in challenge.

Dr. Hunka apologized.

"That's better," 𐒻𐒼𐓂 said. "If you go out with my grandson I will forgive you fully."

The doctor blushed.

"𐒻𐒼𐓂, c'mon," I protested.

After that, they discussed 𐒻𐒼𐓂's health and I stayed out of it. Eventually, Dr. Hunka shook 𐒻𐒼𐓂's hand. I stood with her and she asked if she could speak to me outside the room. I nodded.

"As I was saying," she spoke low, "being in the processed air of the ship will at least buy some time. If she stays.... Well, it's advanced. Does she still smoke? She listed that she used to."

"Not that I know of," I said. "Didn't even know she used to."

"Well, that's something. But still, every breath she takes will just add to the damage. The particulate, the heat, the dryness, it all adds up. She might have a year or only months. Hard to say. No matter what, it'll be significantly less if she stays. She should stay here as long as she will. We have decent filtration."

I nodded. There wasn't much to say after that, and we both found ourselves looking up at the TV. 𐒼𐒷𐓆𐒻𐒼𐒰 flinched and there were a few cries from offscreen as gatorade bottles and beer cans flew in to clatter on the stage. The camera panned over to show a few lifted pickup trucks idling behind the press. Okies in the beds beneath Confederate flags held signs as they shouted. "Leave Ungrateful Injuns," one said. "Go back to your RED Planet," said another. One simply said, "Git!"

"Hey, doc," I said, whispering because by now 𐒻𐒼𐓂 had to be eavesdropping. "About the ship... are you going?"

"Me?" She shook her head.

"Why not?" She was exactly the kind of person the move would need. Educated, athletic, with vital skills. A homegrown celebrity. I knew of a few with questionable tribal affiliation who had made it onto the manifest just by having similar resumés.

"This is my home, you know?" she said, shrugging. "Earth's like a patient. Sick, but not dead yet."

The thing about ecology is it's not any one piece that matters. It's about the system. About how everything interacts and balances out. For the last 70 or so years, that's mostly meant figuring out how to reduce the impact of humans on every other living thing around them. And, in most of those cases, it's been trying to correct previous failed interventions through yet further interventions. A cascade of mistakes. Western science was scrambling to catch up to the Indigenous knowledge that had thrived on the Americas for hundreds of years before the settlers came and tried to wipe it all out.

I could calculate the numbers reasonably well. I could say we need this many buffalo, this many acres of graze, that many rodents, insects, coyotes, foxes. We could expect to cull this many animals each year, leading to this much high quality protein in addition to the aquaponic agriculture and insect yield. I had already done this. We had a team, but since I was the mammal specialist, much of the calculations originated with me. Numbers can be misleading when trying to find the best balance of an entire system, though. Sometimes the right 20 individuals are worth more than 50 random ones.

Ma was one of the right individuals. She was equal to ten younger cows. We needed her. So her final checkup before she was to be finalized and prepped for transport felt like anything but routine.

It helped to keep my mind off the notification I'd gotten an hour earlier from the launch office. The one that said my paperwork had been accepted. My spot reserved. I hadn't signed anything, but I knew who had.

I stood with Nik and several of the ranch hands and veterinary staff and looked down on Ma and Jess from outside her stall. It was just a checkup, I told myself. A formality.

Jess knelt next to Ma's prone form panting heavy in the hay. She lifted a bottle and plugged a syringe into it. Drew out the clear liquid, flicked it. Pressed until a stream geysered up from the finger-length needle. Ma's breathing steadied. It seemed like I could see the coldness of the dose flow through her.

"She's not as young as she used to be," Jess said, rising from the straw. "If we want to be sure, we should monitor her for another day or two."

She pulled the nitrile gloves from her hands, closed the stall door, and leaned back against it.

Nik stepped forward. "You and I both know we don't need to monitor her, we need to replace her."

Jess shook her head.

"Can we just admit this is sentimental, if not downright stupid?" he asked.

I clenched and unclenched my hands. It was enough that Nik was bringing kids around trying to manipulate folks, but today his goddamn voice was suddenly too much for me.

"Nik, stop," Jess said.

"Hell," he had to go on. "Maybe, and this is just me using my damn brain here, we give her spot to an actual person even."

It didn't matter that he was talking about Ma, he was looking sideways at me. Because I hadn't rushed to accept his offer. Hadn't responded at all.

"She's dead weight. Way too much of that in this plan—"

I hit him as hard as I could. He stumbled against the stall but didn't fall.

Two ranch hands had me before I could make another move. "Shut up, Nik. Just shut up." I growled. Nik wiped his mouth with the back of his wrist.

"Jesus, get a goddamn grip," Jess yelled, stepping between us.

"Not bad," he said to me. He stood up, dusted off his hat before putting it on. "Don't change facts, though."

Seeing that Nik didn't want to swing back, the hands let me go.

I pointed. "You check her for rat poison or pesticides or anything? How do we know he isn't making room for a mess of in-laws?"

It was Jess who hit me then. Open palm slap, then she was up in my face. "Now *you* shut up."

Nik stepped forward, put a hand on Jess's arm gently.

"It's okay, Jess. We do stupid things when the fear is in us." He held my gaze but didn't return my glare. "Say stupid things. Lotta uncertainty to get scared of these days. Hard on everyone. I let it get to me too sometimes. Not proud of that. But he knows I love these damn animals. Even, maybe especially, that old bag in there. Knows I would die for them, ain't that right?"

I looked down. I'd seen him ride off after poachers more than once. Seen him work through the hottest days, tempting a goring from the testiest of the bulls to get the herd moved. Damn him for being right.

"Lotta goodbyes being said these days," he kept going. His words landing harder than any counterpunch. "He knows I already signed the papers. Already had to have the hard conversations with the in-laws. Don't he. Yeah, he knows it. See? Knows the way, in the end, that they had to get stern with my wife, same way I might be getting stern with him right now. They had to make her get her focus right. Get it on the future, not the past. Made her vow to make it as good as possible for our boys. Even if it's hard. Even if it's scary. Hold too tight to the past, it'll just drag you under. Hold you down. He knows all that. Ain't that right?"

I didn't know all that. But then I did, too. I shrugged away from everyone and headed out of the barn. I had to get to the hospital.

Instead, I went to the old creekbed where I used to look for turtles and praying mantises as a kid. It was just a dry trough now. I started walking one direction and told myself I would turn around when I hit water or I figured out what to say to ᏂᏦᎤ. By dusk, I had had to give up on both objectives. There was no water, just cracked red soil and bleached white bones. No answers, just the pall of a loss that felt not singular, but constant and ongoing. A single message from ᏂᏦᎤ waited for me on my phone when I got back to my car. "Come on over and see me already," it said.

At the hospital, I passed Doc Hunka on the way to ᏂᏦᎤ's room. We nodded to each other. I wondered if she ever left.

"ᏧᏁᏍᎧ, ᏂᏦᎤ," I said when I entered, but the room was empty.

"She's out back," Dr. Hunka leaned in the doorway. "Forgot to pass that along when I saw you."

Outside, in a lawn chair, head leaned back to look up into the sky, ᏂᏦᎤ was sipping another cup of grape juice.

"ᏧᏁᏍᎧ, ᏂᏦᎤ," I said again. I fell into the seat next to her.

"Rough day?" she asked.

"Yeah."

She hummed an acknowledgement. Took a swig from her juice and looked up into the sky. Eventually, she took my hand in hers and gave it a squeeze.

I pressed my eyes, pinched the bridge of my nose. I pulled up a file on my phone. It was a doubles match from an early 2000s Wimbledon. I had been collecting recordings for the trip. "I know you like men's better," I said. "But all the forums say this one is a match for the ages."

"Oh, those Williams sisters!" She slapped her thigh. "They were really something."

We let the tennis take over. Huddled around a small square light beneath the stars, I didn't know how to begin, and she apparently didn't feel the need to, so we didn't talk. She used to make fun of people who felt the need to occupy silence with empty words. It exhausted her. Me too. I guess I got that from her. Some days we just did this. And after an hour or so, she would get up and say "Good chat."

There were serves, volleys, slams. It was an incredible show of dominance. The sisters flowed like a dance. Like they were the two hands of a single tennis god. On a particularly good point, 𐒻𐓥𐓪 would snap the fingers of her free hand and whoop so loud I knew that the nurses heard it inside at their station.

At some point in the second set, I gave up being mad and took her hand in mine. It was warm, despite the chill in the air.

Before the match was over, 𐒻𐓥𐓪 leaned over and said, "Your momma would be proud."

I hung my head.

𐒻𐓥𐓪 patted my hand. "It'll be okay," she said.

My breath caught. "I—"

"You can't stay," she said. "And I can't go. It's same as it always was."

"But I can't leave you." My voice cracked. I couldn't help but imagine her alone, condition declining. Scared, sad, empty, same as I had been when mom passed away. She would need me like I had needed her.

"I'll be with you," she said. "I'll be closer to you up there than I would be if you were down here. You just gotta have the strength to wait for me."

She let me have some time to compose myself.

"My spaceman. Know your 𐒻𐓥𐓪 will always look over you, ϟ∩ƻOᲂϷΛ. Now, why don't you put on another good match?"

"Thanks, 𐒻𐓥𐓪." I bit the inside of my cheek. Then I raised my phone and searched for another classic from the ones I'd collected.

"But before you get it started,"—she leaned in and held her plastic cup up—"go tell that doctor I'm ready for her to slip me more of the merlot she's got."

Months later, I stood at one of the observation viewports, a few invaluable sprigs of cedar ready. In the central atrium of the ship, buffalo grazed in the reduced gravity. The calves bounded, testing how high they could frolic while the adults just tried to walk as normally as they could. (Though Ma seemed more like the calves than not, delighted by the reduced load on her joints.) Insects lazed through the air, beating their wings out of habit rather than need. A coyote secreted away a mole it had caught. The ship's lifeforce was a steady thrum in the soles of my feet and a nagging pressure at the inside of my ears.

Outside, the black of space enveloped the ship. The stars were everywhere, like a handful of coarse white sand spread across a dead TV screen. The yellow glow of the sun pursued us. Mars glowed red, silently stewing, just slightly aft and above our path.

She had told me not to say goodbye. "We don't say goodbye," she told me. "Say 'until next time.'" So that's what I'd said.

"Now say it like you mean it," she said.

So I did.

Now, before I get rotated off a wake cycle for a rest period, I come here. This is a 𐓷𐓘𐓻𐓘𐓻𐓟 ship, a 𐓡𐓘𐓤𐓘 𐓤𐓘𐓡𐓧𐓪͘𐓵𐓟 𐓰𐓘 𐓨𐓘𐓸𐓟 𐓘𐓤𐓘𐓡𐓘𐓰𐓘[10], and so it is unlike anything that has come before. Through a door next to the viewport, there is a room built for the use of sacred smoke. There's no true sunrise out here, but that doesn't mean we don't still have messages to send to our ancestors.

I find Cassiopeia. I count her major stars. There are actually 26 in total, all more visible here than they were on Earth, but only five major ones that 𐓩𐓤𐓪 and I had keyed in on.

"Alpha, Beta, Gamma, Delta, Epsilon," I name them aloud. Today, there are six. "Hmm."

I count again, making sure my eyes are not playing tricks on me. That I'm not just seeing what I want to see.

"I'll be with you," she'd said. "We're a sky people. When we pass, we return. So no matter what, I'll be with you."

10. HAHnka.KahLOntheh.Da.MAHn.xeh.AHgahahdah. An eagle that travels through the sky/upper world into tomorrow.

"Alpha, Beta, Gamma, Delta, Epsilon," I say. I press my hand to the window. "And you."

Author's Note

Language is sovereignty. I am grateful to *Reckoning* for making it possible to publish the text with Osage (𐓷𐓘𐓻𐓘𐓻𐓟) orthography as originally written. For nonfluent readers, I have included phonetics in the footnotes so you can hear the beauty of language, even as you may not be able to read it. The most fantastical and unbelievable element of this story is that I have written characters decades in the future who speak 𐓷𐓘𐓻𐓘𐓻𐓟 𐓨𐓟 at the same infantile level I do now. This is representative of only my own clumsy competencies. The Osage Language Department and our elders have ensured that ours will be a different linguistic future than depicted here with their incredible dedication and efforts.

Dan Musgrave was raised by animals in rural Kansas. He is a graduate of the University of Missouri-St. Louis MFA, the Odyssey Writing Workshop (2016), and was a member of the Tulsa Artist Fellowship's initial cohort of writing fellows. His writing has appeared in or is forthcoming from *The Sun*, *The Missouri Review*, *New Letters*, *Electric Literature*, *Longreads*, and elsewhere. He is a registered member of the Osage (𐓏𐓘𐓻𐓘𐓻𐓟) Nation.

Where the Water Came From

Jeff Hewitt

The agent assured Tyrel it was a good contract. Eighty-five years wasn't bad, as far as these things went. Could be worse. They could be sending him to Amarok, or Ragnar, or some other red dwarf gravity hell.

Not that Tyrel had much of a choice. More people arrived at the camp every day: dusty, desperate, dropped by coyotes at the border. He remembered his family's long slog from California. One way or another, they had to get out. Just like everybody else.

The sponsorship agent told him about Hallex Industries. How they'd been the government's top orbital vendor for the past thirty years. How, after the Declaration, they were tasked with refugee processing in the Northwest. He told Tyrel about the new seasteads. The state-of-the-art accommodations, just off shore. He told him about the desalination plants, ensuring his loved ones would never go through this again. He did have loved ones, right? People who relied on him?

Tyrel nodded. His wife, their kids, his parents.

The agent smiled, as if their shell-shocked trip through the desert had been serendipitous. What luck, to have an opportunity like this fall into their laps!

But water wars hardly felt like luck to Tyrel.

Then the agent explained the infopacks. Using their patented biomonitors, Hallex would track his dependents' most important milestones. In-house specialists would produce snapshots of their lives, beaming updates to the ship throughout his journey. Despite the lost years and interstellar distances, it would be like Tyrel had been there all along.

Except, of course, he wouldn't be. He'd be frozen in cryogenic goo, hurtling toward Epsilon Eridani.

Volunteering for a trillionaire's interstellar boondoggle wasn't on Tyrel's bucket list. Neither was abandoning his family. But what could he do? Martial law had been declared. It was only a matter of time before the camps became funnels for the meat grinder. At least Hallex gave them a chance.

Was he sure he wanted to do this? The agent reminded him this was an all-or-nothing deal.

Tyrel didn't want to do this. But he felt like he had to. For the kids' sake.

He nodded.

"Great. Now, just state your name for the scanner, then the names of your dependents. Then we'll work through the rest."

Tyrel looked into the battery of lenses. He tried to keep his voice from shaking.

"Tyrel Brand. My parents, Erik Brand and Anya Teagan. My wife . . . ." The tears came. "My wife, Lexi Brand. My son, Jordan. And my daughter, Emery."

Tyrel had a week to say goodbye.

After the biometrics, the behavioral panels, the skills assessments, and the corporate orientation, they shipped Tyrel to Kiribati. He and a dozen other passing grades stepped onto the Hallex elevator.

The burly guy next to Tyrel nudged him.

"Ever been up before?"

Tyrel shook his head, watching palm trees become dots against the seafoam below. Burly grunted.

"Change your damn life."

But Tyrel's life had already changed.

Emi had begged him to stay, clawing the logo on his new jumpsuit as Lexi pulled her away. She screamed as the repurposed troop carrier touched down behind them. Its rotors churned dust across the camp, wind whipping Lexi's hair.

Jordan stayed back with his grandparents, staring from their tent. He'd been sullen. Quiet. Old enough to hide his grief, but not old enough to face it.

Tyrel kissed his wife. He smoothed her hair, salt stinging his tongue. Maybe there was a time when they would have fought this. Would have faced down war and famine to stay together.

Maybe. But things had changed. She'd wanted to leave after

the first attack on the lithium mine, but Tyrel convinced her to stay. It was a good job. They couldn't let some desert crazies ruin that. Besides, the Guard had been called in. They'd settle things down.

Tyrel had never been more wrong.

Then Emi had screeched, inches from Tyrel's face. He wiped the tears from Lexi's cheeks and let go. His parents waved as he slipped into the dust cloud, Emi's scream still ringing in his ear.

"Look at that."

Burly again, the blue curve of Earth glinting in his eyes. He pointed to something above them. A fleet of docked ships, their long spines and armored sides like wingless dragonflies against the black of space.

"Crazy."

Tyrel agreed.

They separated the men from the women. Not that there were many women. But eighty-five years was a long time. If anything went wrong, the *Bounty* couldn't handle more cargo. Cargo, in this case, meant people. Hallex Industries' "beneficiaries."

Of course, nothing would go wrong. The Hallex people assured them of that.

Cryo-pods lined the walls of the ship, status lights and access ports glowing against sheer metal. A technician explained how they'd fill up with a kind of artificial amniotic fluid, shielding them from acceleration and keeping them alive. Anyone outside the pods during their maser assist wouldn't make it more than a few seconds.

"So, unless you want to end up an eighty-five-year-old puddle, stay calm, and don't abort when the chamber fills."

He walked them through a few scenarios: pod failure, waking up, lock-in. None of which would happen, of course. Then he opened it up to questions.

"Will we dream?" Tyrel heard himself ask.

"We're, uh . . . not sure, actually."

The pods maintained a minor level of brain activity. There might be something like dreaming. But it probably wouldn't be eighty-five years of lucid fantasies. Next question.

Tyrel never thought of himself as much of a dreamer. But he kept feeling like he was about to wake up.

Sometime later, Hallex's trillionaire founder shook Tyrel's hand. He'd given a speech, telling them all how important they were, how he hoped to join them, how they'd write brave new histories amongst the stars. Tyrel doubted that.

The next day, a Hallex rep shuffled Tyrel into a media bay. A holo winked on as the door closed.

It was a farewell message. Lexi sat on a grey couch with Emi on her lap, Tyrel's parents on either side. A spotless kitchen gleamed behind them, hints of an ocean view through its window, an empty cushion where Jordan should be.

"Hi, Tyrel."

"Daddy!"

"We just wanted to—"

"Come home, Daddy! We got new bedrooms, and—"

"Honey, let Mommy—"

"No!" Emi squeaked. "I want to talk to Daddy!"

Lexi nodded, bouncing Emi on her knee. She distracted her with a pack of gummies.

"We just wanted. . . ." Lexi trailed off, eyes unfocused. "I'm sorry, I—"

She passed Emi to Tyrel's mom and walked off-screen, hand over her mouth. His dad nodded to the camera. The feed cut out.

Then Tyrel's cryo-pod was filling with cold, oxygenated fluid. The viscous goo rose past his ankles, his knees, hugging his skin. He knew he didn't need to hold his breath, but he couldn't help it.

When he woke up—if he woke up—everything he ever knew would be gone.

When Jordan was younger, Tyrel would take him out past Slab City to ride the dunes. They'd throw their fat-wheeled e-bikes in the truck and park on the wash, riding up and down the hills, watching the Salton Sea recede, sunset after perfect sunset.

That was before the water shortages. Before the crazies started blowing things up.

Tyrel wasn't sure if he'd dreamt. But after he hacked up the last of the fluid, those memories kept playing in the back of his mind. Like he'd been reliving them for decades.

He struggled to the railing, muscles straining under his weight. According to the technician, they'd done something to keep them toned. It didn't feel like it.

Where was the tech, anyway?

Pods hissed open as more beneficiaries woke up. A few stayed closed, occupants still blissfully unaware. Burly stretched out a few pods down. He cracked his neck and wrung his hair, globs of cryo goo splatting the floor.

Something was off. But eighty-five years of sleep fogged Tyrel's brain.

Then it hit him: gravity. They weren't supposed to have gravity.

The bulkhead door slid open. A woman in black stood beside one of the Hallex captains, hair slicked back, holo tab pulled up in front of her. Neither looked happy.

"If I could have everyone's attention." The captain boomed. "There have been some . . . changes you should all be aware of."

Eighty-five years was a long time. Of course things would change. But Tyrel didn't expect this.

An orbital ring rotated above the auditorium's geodesic skylights, ships studding its surface. The Bounty was there, spinning away, hull dwarfed by the ring's size. Dozens of other stations dotted the void, bathed in pale orange light. A lavender-tinged planet loomed below. Sunrise painted a crescent along its surface. Aurorae rippled its atmosphere.

They'd taken Tyrel and his fellow beneficiaries—"survivors," people kept whispering—to a processing center. They gave them new jumpsuits. Some black, some red, some a color Tyrel wanted to call teal, but Lexi would call turquoise. New logos graced their chests: Almani, Edict Engineering, Sojourner Orbital. More colors, more logos. Sorting them into groups. Someone gave Tyrel a cup of frothy liquid and made him drink it. Then they herded him and the rest of the survivors into an auditorium.

Burly sat in the front row, spilling over his seat. He scanned the room, smiled when he saw Tyrel.

"Hey. Same team." Burly pulled on his logo patch. They'd been drafted into something called Ichor Hydro. Light blue.

Tyrel wanted to smile, but he couldn't. He wanted to wake up back in California, before everything went to shit.

The woman who supervised their transfer walked on stage. Chatter died down as a logo appeared behind the podium. Minimal arabesques surrounded a purple globe, a river carving through it.

"Not what you expected, eh?"

Murmurs rippled through the auditorium, her attempt at humor falling flat.

"My name's Liya Chaudhary. I'm the presiding chair of the Tiānti Consortium, representing Chakra Subatomics. I'm sure you all. . . ."

Chaudhary paused. She'd clearly prepared for this. But confronted with a thousand hungry faces, she balked.

"Listen. I know this is fucked. We're not the only system dealing with this. So just bear with me."

The crowd fidgeted as she got them up to speed.

Hallgier Crow—the founder of Hallex—was dead. Which wasn't that surprising; not even trillionaires live forever. Twenty years later, his company followed suit. Now, the Consortium had to deal with something called "contract transposition." Hence all the new jumpsuits.

But the end of Hallex was just the beginning. Thirty-five years after the *Bounty*'s departure—or sometime between now and yesterday for Tyrel—some genius at Sojourner invented something called a "scalar field drive," shortening the trip to Eridani to about forty minutes. Add another fifty years, and the desolate ball of ice they were meant to settle had already been colonized. And recolonized. And turned into a research outpost. And then colonized again.

By the end of the presentation, people's eyes had glazed over. Not from boredom, but something else: something between information overload and disbelief, utter confusion and learned helplessness. It was the same combination that pushed many of them here in the first place. Eighty-five years later, and they were still wondering how it had come to this.

Tyrel felt his temperature rising. He'd sacrificed everything, betting on a better life for his kids. But it turned out to be just that. A bet. With no guarantees.

He'd signed the contract. Did everything he'd been told. He didn't want "transposition." He wanted to see his family.

Tyrel stood on his chair.

"What about the infopacks?" He shouted, mind reeling.

What Tyrel meant to say was: What about my wife? My parents? What about Jordan and Emery? But the contract had reduced them to a string of data points he might never see.

Chaudhary blinked, grappling with the question. She checked the podium and it clicked.

"Yes... The infopacks. We have a plan for—"

But it was too late. Other survivors leapt to their feet, bellowing questions, pitch rising to riot levels. Chaudhary pulled a mask from her pocket. She slipped it on, signaling someone off-stage.

Only then did Tyrel notice the security drones unfolding around the auditorium. The ventilation kicked on as unorganized groups tried to force their way on stage. Others made for the exits, bodies piling up as they fought to get out.

A riot squad entered from backstage. Tyrel saw Chaudhary point him out as he lost his balance, collapsing to the floor.

But Tyrel felt fine. Whatever they'd spiked the air with told him everything was going to be fine. The only thing that nagged him, that followed him down as he blacked out, was a high-pitched ringing in his ear.

Tyrel shot awake. His stomach ached. Dawn peeked through the windows, crimson light silhouetting the nearest bunks. A few others stirred, getting ready for work.

He'd been on Jal a couple weeks now. But he kept relieving those first chaotic hours: The frenzy on the orbital. Waking up as they landed. Shuffling through the unexpected city, twinkling in Jal's early summer. The workers' lodging. Another batch of tests and training.

The dorms were basic. Low-slung warehouses with corrugated siding, stuffed with beds, communal bathrooms, and two kitchens. Tyrel shared his with a hundred-odd Ichor conscripts. He headed to the bathroom, jumpsuit rolled under his arm. His stomach was still adjusting to the planet's microflora. That frothy drink had prompted a few days of explosive diarrhea. But without it, he wouldn't have made it a week.

Burly leaned over one of the sinks, tweezing hairs from his beard. He nodded to Tyrel.

"Big day."

Tyrel nodded back. It was a big day. He squatted over the frigid metal toilet, thoughts vaulting past his work shift. He had his first conciliation tonight.

The Tiānti Conciliation Protocol dealt with the unique problems the survivors posed. Rather than dump eighty-five years of infopacks on them, the content would be released piecemeal. Probably edited too, Tyrel thought. But he'd take what he could get.

Each week, a hundred survivors got their fifteen minutes in a viewing suite, followed by mandatory group therapy. Just enough to keep them sane. To keep some hope alive as they adjusted. Maybe it would help, dealing with this together. Whatever "this" was.

They'd already seen what could happen if they stepped out of line.

After a dissociative shift at Ichor's water treatment plant, Tyrel and Burly caught the bus into Sheen. The city had an official name. Something in the local pidgin. But everyone called it "Sheen." Just like they called the planet "Jal," even though it was listed as "Skadi" when Tyrel signed up.

They all had meanings. Histories. But they meant nothing to Tyrel.

The bus trundled over the dirt road, winding along the bay. Sheen stood at the outlet of a glacial valley, the city sprouting from alien tundra, framed by icy mountains, aurorae dancing overhead. Squat autofabs hunched next to multi-story farm towers. A street grid had formed during Tyrel's lost decades, the Consortium's headquarters at its center.

The bus stopped to let a line of construction vehicles pass. Tyrel turned to Burly. He stared across the quiet ocean, past the icebergs that never melted.

"What will you do while we . . . ."

While they did what? Reviewed their family trees?

Burly shrugged, arms crossed over his gut.

"Said I could surf the net. Guess they got something setup."

His name was Cedro, but Tyrel still called him Burly. He'd gotten to know him down at the plant. They'd both worked in hydraulics, more or less: Tyrel in lithium flashing, Burly in shale. He guessed that was why the algorithm put them with Ichor, the planet's water and hydrogen monopoly.

Ironic, Tyrel thought. It was water—or the lack thereof—that put them here. But Burly represented an odd minority: the people that signed up with Hallex not for their families, but because they had nothing else.

"Let me know what you find." Tyrel said.

"También."

The bus parked in front of a rec center in Hazar, Sheen's pedestrian district. A Consortium welcoming party stood in formation off the road. Tyrel spotted Chaudhary, checking her watch inside.

A conciliator led Tyrel to some temporary buildings out back. Repurposed containers. The kind that went up and down the planet's lone elevator across the bay. They passed security guards at each door, eventually entering one of the stacked prefabs.

"Here we are. Brand. Suite eleven."

She scanned his face and the door opened. A folding chair waited in front of a holo terminal. Soundproofing padded the walls.

"I'll grab you when you're done." The conciliator smiled and walked out.

Tyrel sat. A play button appeared, the old Hallex logo rotating behind it.

Tyrel hesitated. For him, it had only been a few weeks. How

many years had they compressed into fifteen minutes? For the first time, he wondered if he wanted to see this at all.

But he pressed play. The Hallex logo expanded, revealing a flat blue seascape, a jagged spire rising from Puget Sound. Some promo for the seastead. Tyrel swept through the corporate fluff. He froze when he saw his wife and kids, back on that grey couch. A date notched the corner of the image, a ticker noting the time since Tyrel had left.

+00:01:03:22:18

Emery sleeps, splayed across Lexi's chest. Jordan plays a game at the other end of the couch. Light flickers over their faces as they watch something, Jordan pretending not to, Lexi lost in it.

The view shifts to the other side of the room. A live feed shows the Bounty whipping past Saturn, magsails extended.

+00:01:17:04:53

Emery alone on the couch. Maritime clouds fill the windows.

"Hi, Daddy."

Tyrel balled a hand over his mouth.

"They told me that anytime I want to talk to you, I can just talk, and you'll get it. Eventually."

She seemed so much older already. Her eyes had changed. They saw the distance between them, the unbridgeable gulf of time that would forever keep them apart.

"I just wanted to say I miss you. And—"

"Come on, Emi! We're late."

+00:02:05:10:39

Surveillance footage shows his parents walking through a park. They stop at a railing to gaze across the wind-swept sound.

+00:02:18:23:51

Lexi on the couch. She puts her hair up, pushes her fingers into the bags under her eyes. She searches for something to say, then shakes her head. "Sorry. This is too weird."

+00:03:01:08:07

Jordan sits on the coffee table. Bruises mottle his chin, a black ring around one eye.

"I hate it here. I. . . ." His lip quivers as a tear drips down his cheek. He wipes it away. "I can't believe you did this to us. The only reason I'm doing this stupid video is because the shrink made me. And they track everything, so. . . ."

Still mad, Tyrel thought. Eighty-five years, and he's still a teenager. Maybe Jordan would always be a teenager to him.

The more Tyrel thought about that, the less he liked it.

The lights in the gymnasium whined, just above the ringing in Tyrel's ear. The conciliator—the same woman who'd shown him to his suite—scanned their circle of folding chairs. Her eyes landed on Tyrel.

"Mr. Brand. Would you like to share?"

Tyrel shook his head. But he knew she would make him say something.

"It just . . . doesn't feel real."

Jordan had gone on: saying he'd never forgive him, that he'd never do another video. Tyrel figured that was just teenage angst. It had to be, right?

Burly and Tyrel waited in line for the bus back to Ichor.

"I didn't know where to begin. The sites are all different."

"Makes sense." Tyrel watched people file onto the next bus. Red jumpsuits. Edict Engineering.

"The whole system's different. The 'NL-net.' Some quantum shit from that lady's company." He meant Chaudhary, who'd just flown off. "Like Earth's just a different time zone."

Why not? Tyrel thought. Eighty-five years.

The bus left. Another jostled up the road, headlights throwing erratic shadows through the fleshy, blue-black plants that dotted the tundra.

"So, what's new?

Burly grunted. "Everything. Nothing. New wars. Old people. Another sexy blue alien franchise. Found some articles about us and the Tau Ceti people, though."

"Really?" Somehow, that surprised Tyrel. Who would miss them?

"Yeah. There's this charity—"

Suddenly, an Ichor guy bolted from the back of the line. He barreled through a security guard, tumbling, then scrambling into the road. People shouted as he sprinted past, closing on the approaching bus and—

Gravel scraped under the bus's tires as it braked, followed by a sickly crunch. The man screamed. And kept screaming.

The bus had swerved. But not soon enough to save the would-be suicide's legs. Guards and conciliators rushed toward him. In the commotion, Tyrel recognized the agonized face as one of the men from his circle.

There are five basic steps to water treatment. The first is coagulation: dispersing charged ions to bind any dissolved particles. Second is flocculation: mixing the water, letting it form "flocs"—clumps of all the crap you don't want. Next comes sedimentation: letting it all settle to the bottom. Then filtration: a series of molecular membranes sieve out the leftovers. Finally, disinfection: blasting the filtered water with UV light, hopefully killing whatever made it through the other steps.

Especially important on an alien planet, Tyrel thought.

Jal's short summer had waned once again. The spiky, blue-black anthos bloomed along the roadsides, flower stalks bending under their own weight, purple spores hanging on the air. Ice crept down the mountainsides, lavender snow algae streaking their rocky faces.

Tyrel sighed and descended into the sedimentation pond. Ichor had him and Burly working overtime, processing as much water as possible before the bay froze over. The same thing, every winter. The workload meant the ponds—huge concrete trenches by the bay—got clogged up more than usual. So, they had to empty them out and mop up all the shit. Which humans apparently still did better than machines.

Cheaper, anyway, Tyrel thought. But at least they got overtime. Extra monopoly money. Better than what the Almani guys got.

Not much had changed on Jal. More paved roads. A couple new buildings. Countless accidents, maiming and killing workers. Tyrel had adapted to its eccentric, ten-month cycle: the long shifts at the plant, the rare days off, puttering around Hazar, the cramped lodging. But he felt like he'd aged decades. God knows his family had.

Jordan had followed through on his threat. Tyrel only ever saw him in the background of Lexi's messages. And then, not even there. Secondhand, Tyrel heard about his son dropping out of school, falling into a gang, then disappearing altogether. Every conciliation, he hoped for news. And every time, he was disappointed.

His parents died a couple years after he'd left. Lung cancer. Probably from toxic dust blown off the Salton Sea. Lexi started messaging more after that, even though she'd moved on. She'd found a job on the seastead, met someone new. Probably would have happened even if Tyrel had stayed.

But Emi . . . Emi was his lifeline. More and more, the conciliations were like conversations with his daughter. It was like she could guess what Tyrel would have said, would have thought. A part of her mind she accessed every time she sat down and talked to him.

Tyrel watched her grow up. From five to twenty-five, in little more than a year. The birthday parties. The first crush. The teenage drama. She got straight A's, went to Stanford, got engaged, called it off. She was smarter than Tyrel ever was. Smarter than he ever would be.

It took a while, but he'd opened up in therapy. He cried. A lot. Not so much in grief like the others, but in hope. Hope for Emi's future. Hope that, despite what he'd done, everything would work out. Life on Jal was bearable with that kind of hope.

At sunset, the skies a deep scarlet impossible on Earth, Burly refilled their assigned pond.

"You thought about what you're going to say?"

Tyrel shrugged, watching the water rise.

"I've been thinking about that since we got here."

There was a charity back on Earth that put Hallex survivors in touch with their descendants, if they could find them. They took applications over the NL-net. But time online wasn't cheap. And bandwidth limited their messages to text. People like Burly—with contractual access—wised up pretty quick, undercutting official rates.

Of course, the Consortium eventually caught on. Protocols had to be followed.

Burly was good for it, though.

Dear Emery,

Where do I start? How do you write a letter to someone you left behind? All I can say is: I miss you. Watching you grow up has been the proudest I've ever felt.

Here on Jal, you're still in your twenties. But if I do the math.... It's hard to even think about. Eighty-five years, like a blink. Maybe you were always the older, wiser one, trying to get me to stay.

Life on Jal is tough. The sun's dimmer. Oranger, too. Our orbit's all lopsided, with long, brutal winters, frost and fleas biting every time you step outside. But the summers are beautiful. Crystal clear rivers gushing into the bay. Auroras in the night sky. I wish you could see the sunsets. Even better than back home.

Hell, maybe you have seen them. Things changed so much while we were under. The people that took over our contracts say we could even go back to Earth, if we pay our dues. But that's just a pipe dream.

Whatever's going on back home, I hope you're making the most of it. That's all I ever wanted. Whatever pain I caused, I was only trying to do what I thought was right. I wanted you and your brother to have a chance, and didn't see any other way.

Maybe I was wrong. But I can't take it back.

I love you. I'm sorry I wasn't there.

—Dad

They rode the bus into Sheen, the road paved with some new synthetic. Workers complained about their pay rates. Someone heard Ichor was paying the women's camp five more erds an hour. Hazard pay, Burly muttered.

No one took the gossip too seriously. But everyone went quiet when the bus pulled into Hazar. Security guards lined the streets. Drones hovered above the intersections.

By the time they reached the rec center, no one wanted to get out.

People shouted across the gym. Conciliators tried to calm anyone who would listen. Riot police dragged out those who wouldn't. Eventually, the mood stabilized enough for Chaudhary to address the crowd.

"Connectivity issues." That was the official line. But the survivors knew they were being taught a lesson: For the black markets popping up across Sheen. For unauthorized use of the NL-net. For the runaways who had set up a village across the bay.

Chaudhary told them that Sojourner and Chakra were working to restore access. In the meantime, they should take this opportunity to work through their frustrations here, in therapy.

That set the crowd off again. A guard nearly knocked Tyrel over, yanking a man out by his jumpsuit, fabric ripping at the seams. Riot shields turned on around the gym.

At moments like these, Tyrel's ear always rang.

The remaining survivors sat in their circles, drones still patrolling the gymnasium. Tyrel scanned the empty seats, then realized the conciliator was staring at him. She'd asked him something.

"Sorry, what?"

"If you could receive another update from Emery, what would it be?"

Tyrel shrugged. He looked at the other dead-eyed group members, lost in their imaginations. Their own missing memories.

"I'd take anything."

The conciliator nodded, like she could sympathize.

"What, specifically, would you like to see?"

What did she want to hear? What was the point of pushing him at a moment like this?

"Just her. Living her life." He finally said. "Making her own choices. Even if they're bad ones. I mean, it's more than we can say." A couple people in his group tuned back in. "Serving out these contracts we never signed, using your fake money in your shitty company stores."

"Now, when I hear you say that, I hear—"

"You don't hear anything." Tyrel blurted, bunching his fists. The whole circle was staring at him now. He noticed the patches they'd made to their suits, unwilling to pay for new ones. "Yeah, you do your job, and you placate, and you act like you understand. But you don't. Because after these sessions, you go back up to your orbital, while the rest of us freeze down here."

A few people murmured, nodding. Tyrel stood.

"We do your grunt work, trapped in debt, while you work us to death."

"Yeah."

"That's right."

Burly looked over from his group. He prodded his neighbors, pointed to Tyrel. The same thing happened in waves across the gym.

"If you could sit down, Mr. Brand, I think we—"

"The only 'we' here is the people sitting down!" The ringing in his ear rose with his voice. He stabbed his finger at the conciliator, knowing it wasn't her fault, but no longer caring. "You drip-feed the infopacks to keep us in line, doling out erds to blow in Hazar...."

A drone started towards him, riot squad trailing.

"The truth is, we'll never fulfill our contracts. We'll never go back to Earth, even though we could. We'll never see—"

A guard grabbed his arm. Tyrel resisted.

"None of this works without us!"

They dragged him from the circle, struggling.

"Without us—"

The drone tapped his neck and everything went black.

They kept him in iso for two days, that first time. It wouldn't be the last.

As winter set in, word of the "connectivity issues"—and Tyrel's outburst—spread; first through the dorm, then Ichor, then Almani. Pretty soon, Edict guys were stopping him in the street, telling him they agreed with what he was saying. Tyrel wasn't sure what he was saying himself.

He and Burly spent their days at a distillery behind the ladies' barracks, fighting off loneliness and the swarming snow fleas. When they weren't doing that, they cracked ice and replaced pipes, which exploded during the coldest months. Tyrel kept writing letters to Emi. Not that he could send them.

If people asked, Tyrel gave them a piece of his mind: Pay was a joke. They might as well be slaves. And the Consortium had weaponized the infopacks. What kind of soulless automaton would do that? The only solution was to stop working. General strike.

Tiānti goons grabbed him again in Hamsa—the long month in the middle of winter. But this time, instead of throwing him in iso, they took him up the elevator, then shuttled him back to where this whole nightmare started. An escort led him past the auditorium, into an office the size of their dorm. A window screen covered one wall. Jal hung below, ice reflecting the flickering orange of Eridani.

Liya Chaudhary sat behind a large desk at the far side of the room. Tyrel checked for guards, for drones, for any kind of security. He didn't see any.

"You're turning into a bit of a troublemaker." Chaudhary sighed, eyes still glued to her desk holo.

Tyrel walked over to one of the grey armchairs by her desk, felt the rough, printed upholstery. Chaudhary turned off her holo.

"Please." She gestured toward the chair.

"What is this?" Tyrel asked.

"Some fabric Almani's testing. Anthos-derived."

"I mean: what am I doing here?"

"I think you know the answer to that."

Tyrel snorted. "Yeah. Right."

He went over to the wall projection, put his hand through the curve of the planet below. Little reflections wrapped around his fingers. Like his whole life was another image. Another infopack.

"Like hell froze over."

Chaudhary had snuck up behind him.

"What?" Tyrel was tired. Confused. Still cold from the bite of Jal's lingering winter.

"My old boss described it that way. Jal."

Tyrel nodded, but then shook his head.

"No. Hell's something you lost and can't get back."

"Hm." Chaudhary thought about that for a moment. "I'm going to be honest with you, Mr. Brand. We're at the edge of civilization out here. A single fault could mean ruin. Not just for you and the other workers, but for everyone."

"That's the line?"

Chaudhary looked at him like he was a petulant child. Or an embarrassing parent.

"The Sojourner people want to strap you to that piece of shit you came in on and send you to Sirius."

Tyrel shrugged. "Then what? Do all this again?"

"I don't think they care about that part. And, frankly, neither do I."

Tyrel turned to face her. But he didn't have anything to say. She wasn't telling him anything new.

Chaudhary smoothed her suit. "Just remember: we can live without you up here. The people on the surface can't say the same."

Intimidation by proxy then, Tyrel thought. All those poor souls left to freeze, just because he wouldn't shut up. But he didn't believe it for a second. He knew where the water came from.

"That's it." Thiba said, leaning in, squinting at the terminal. Tyrel and Burly lingered over her shoulder, clueless.

"Everything?" Tyrel asked.

Thiba nodded, patting the fan-covered box she'd spliced into their network. "Everything in, everything out."

She looks like Burly, Tyrel thought. Big. Maybe that's why he likes her. That, and she runs the distillery.

The strike had held through the winter. But the Consortium's tit-for-tats were getting worse.

At first, it was just the Ichor workers. Then Edict voted to strike, and Tiānti put the whole planet under lockdown. When Almani joined, they tried sealing the farm towers. Of course, it was hard to keep the workers out when they wanted food for the orbitals.

"What about the Hallex archives?"

Thiba tapped in a couple commands, then nodded at the lines on-screen.

"All there."

Burly clasped her shoulders, grinning.

"Nice work, babe."

"Quit calling me 'babe.'"

Thiba tabbed through menus, text strobing. "Looks like you got a message, Ty."

"What?" Tyrel was still thinking about the archives. It had been months since he'd heard anything from Emi.

"From that charity. Tiānti's been sitting on it."

"They would." Tyrel grumbled.

"Want me to read it?"

Mr. Brand:

On behalf of the Interstellar Migrant Workers Alliance, I'd like to thank you for your letter. You and your compatriots are a beacon of hope for thousands of migrant workers across the IS Free Trade Region.

As is often the case in these matters, tracking your next of kin has proven more complicated than initially assessed. While we were able to locate your daughter, we regret to inform you that she passed away three years ago, in Adelaide, F.O. Our team is now attempting to contact her surviving children.

Our sincerest condolences for your loss. Know that you are not alone, and we will continue searching for your next of kin. Please let us know if there is anything we can do to support you in the meantime.

Stay strong,
Shiraz Davani
SVP, Survivor Outreach
IMWA

Something broke inside Tyrel when he read those words. No doubt Emi had lived a long, beautiful life, retiring in what he guessed was Australia. But to him, she still had everything ahead of her.

He couldn't bring himself to watch the rest of the infopacks, knowing what he knew. Now, all he had was the cause.

With spring around the corner, stored water was running low on the orbitals. And with their reclamators acting up, Tyrel knew they couldn't last long. He denied Tiānti's claims of sabotage. The Sojourner survivors had finally joined the strike. Deferred maintenance was just an unfortunate byproduct.

The Consortium still refused to negotiate. But the workers stayed united.

"Shunto." That's what the people in Jiyu called it. The spring offensive.

Tyrel watched the town's children play at the edge of an empty field. Frost crunched beneath their woven boots. Scarves flapped from their necks. No one seemed bothered by the cold in Jiyu—the free city on the other side of the bay.

Oto, Jiyu's nominal leader, pointed to a poisonous green vein on the mountainside above.

"They started dumping a few weeks ago. Runoff from the new builds by the elevator."

"They're desperate."

"Maybe. But if that leeches into the ground water, we'll lose the crops. We can't last another winter without them."

Tyrel glanced back to the cut-stone houses and open-air markets of Jiyu. Chopped anthos smoked beneath racks of fish, plumes billowing into the steel sky. A young woman ran towards them, waving her arms, shouting something Tyrel couldn't make out. He still had a hard time understanding the locals.

Would he ever feel at home here? It wasn't like he could go back; he'd lost his real home before they ever left.

Oto grabbed his arm.

"She says they're demolishing the dorms."

They took the town's fastest boat down the coast. When they got to the Ichor complex, they found security teams battling residents, attempting to clear the dorms. Bunkbeds burned in a line around the building. Mobile autofabbers formed a perimeter on the far side, demolition plows rigged up and ready to go.

Tyrel sprinted into the fray, looking for Burly. Rocks flew through the air, forcing the security teams back. He found Burly fighting off three guards at once, easily throwing two of them to the ground. The final guard drew his stun gun, then froze, recognizing Tyrel.

"Why?" Was all Tyrel could shout. How could this be worth it?

The guard backed away, muttering something into his helmet. The rest followed, survivors chucking ripped-out fixtures after them. Burly wiped the sweat and soot from his face. Blood trickled from a swollen lip.

"Guess that's all it takes for you, huh?"

Residents crowded around Tyrel, screaming past the autofabbers, throwing whatever they could find at the regrouping security teams. Oto appeared, pulling at his elbow.

"We must go. Find you a place to hide."

But Tyrel couldn't go. He'd seen how the residents rallied. How the guards froze when they recognized him.

Tyrel never planned on becoming a leader. But that's what he was to the survivors. Someone who wouldn't sit down and take it. He grabbed Oto's shoulder.

"Tell everyone what's happening. Everyone. Go!"

Oto frowned, nodded, and ran off.

Tyrel took stock of the remaining Ichor workers. Solemn faces nodded back, ash staining their worn-out uniforms. He turned to Burly.

"What now?"

Burly crooked his arm, holding it out to Tyrel. He smiled.

It took Tyrel a moment to understand. But when he locked arms with Burly, the rest followed suit. They formed a chain around the building, facing the autofabbers. They gazed through the hulking machines, past the wannabe soldiers, beyond the cruelness of Tiānti and the inconceivable expanse that divided their lives. What they saw was more than fair wages, more than lost memories, more than the struggle of the weak versus the strong. What they saw was hope. The hope that only hardship can provide.

They stood that way for some time. A late-season snow began to fall, sizzling over the fires. The sky dimmed. Security guards fidgeted on the other side of their line.

Then Tyrel heard something. A dull but growing roar, like the winter winds that blew in from the bay. The guards wavered, watching the Ichor residents, then furtively glancing towards Sheen.

"Look!" Someone shouted, pointing up the road.

Voices broke through as Tyrel spotted the mob. Hundreds of people in mismatched uniforms marched across the tundra, brandishing homemade weapons and eighty-five years of pent-up rage. Suddenly, a fireball erupted on the other side of the autofabbers. The riot squad scattered as more explosions rocked the line, the mob cheering as they charged.

They didn't see the machines inching forward, treads chewing through frozen dirt.

The chain faltered as people stepped back, trying to keep their distance. But they held together, watching the plows grind toward them.

They'll stop, Tyrel reassured himself, sweating from the fires. Some basic, inalterable safety feature. But when he thought of all the workers who'd died over the years, he knew that wasn't true.

In that moment, Tyrel made the martyr's choice. He'd lost enough. He wouldn't yield, no matter what the Consortium threatened him with. Besides, he'd given up his life once already.

The chain broke as the autofabbers closed in, residents forfeiting the dorm. Tyrel didn't judge them. Someone had to keep fighting. It just wouldn't be him.

Burly stood by, arm still wrapped in Tyrel's. The plows loomed, tarnished metal rending the ground.

"Run, Burly." Tyrel shouted over the noise.

Burly shook his head, smiling. He turned and hugged Tyrel. He slapped him on the back, tears streaking his face. Then Burly cinched Tyrel's arm, spun him around, and hurled him back toward the dorm.

Tyrel tumbled over the rocky dirt. There was a sound like a giant cracking its knuckles, and everything stopped.

They held the funeral in Jiyu, just outside of town. Looking at the crowd, Tyrel thought all of Sheen had turned out. Unwashed jumpsuits lined the terraced hillside, handmade threads mixed in with frayed corporate monotones. They waited for Tyrel to say a few words.

Did they come for Burly? Or did they come for him? After all, workers died every day on Jal. What made Burly special was that he'd died standing up for something. Standing up for him.

Tyrel stepped up to the altar. A container held Burly's ashes.

"Burly—" His voice caught in his throat. "Sorry. Cedro. I never called him Cedro. Always 'Burly.' Anyone who knew him will know why: he was a big guy. With a low tolerance for bullshit."

Laughter rumbled through the crowd.

"I met Burly back on Earth. He was the only person that talked to me before we got on those cryo-ships. The only one who seemed to know what he was getting himself into. . . ."

Tyrel glanced back to Thiba. She nodded, tears clinging to her eyes.

"Because Burly didn't leave anyone behind. He had no one to leave. More than anyone else, we were Burly's family. You needed something done, and Burly did it. Who wouldn't, for family? Burly—Cedro—never gave it a second thought. He saved me," Tyrel's voice trembled, "without a second thought. And I can't help wondering: what did I ever do for him? What kind of family was I, dwelling on my old life, pining over people I'll never see again?"

Tyrel let that settle over the crowd. He saw how they waited.

How they nodded.

"What kind of family are we?" He asked. "Most of us left Earth in desperation. We didn't come here for ourselves. We came for the people we left behind.

"Yet, here we are, on a cold, strange planet, living together, bathing together, trying to remember a time when we had a home . . . when Burly's home was right here."

A few industrial coughs echoed from the hillside.

"Burly understood that no matter where you are, you find your family there. Because if you don't, you truly have nothing."

A chorus grew among the ranks of onlookers, and Tyrel felt himself letting go. He couldn't go back to save his wife, his kids, his parents. But he could do this. A kind of penance. For Jordan. For Lexi. For Emi and Burly and all the rest.

"If I learned one thing from Burly, it's that we are what we're willing to do for those around us. And what do we do? We toil. We struggle. We've built our homes here, and the Consortium acts like they own our lives. They tell us they own this planet. But without us, there is no Jal. We. Are. Jal!"

The crowd roared and Tyrel roared back, adrenaline wiping his mind as talk of revolution poured out of him.

They scattered Burly's ashes over a field that would soon be cropped. He'd become a part of Jal. Even more than he already was.

Tyrel watched a tiller mix his remains into the soil. A cold, unthinking machine, burying his friend under the frozen dirt. Fitting, he thought.

Teams of survivors headed into Sheen. They tore the beds from their dorms, piled them onto hijacked trucks, and formed a massive pyre at the edge of Jiyu. The Edict chemists handed out the firebombs they'd devised. Revelers tossed them into the jumbled mattresses and frames.

The bonfire lit up the night. Bottles were passed around. People laughed, and danced, and cried.

Tyrel, Thiba, and Oto sat outside a stone hut by the bay, the pale light from Jal's moons glancing off the stippled black water.

They planned. There would be a march, straight into the heart of Sheen. They had to show the Consortium this wasn't a one-off. Some spasm from being pushed too far at the wrong time.

"No more bombs." Tyrel said. They could take the high road. He had to believe, with the IMWA and their contacts on the orbitals, that there were people out there who would support them.

"What about security?" Oto asked.

"What about them?"

"They may have orders. Suppress, at any cost."

Oto had always been the most caring of them, Tyrel thought. Someone people trusted. He was Jal's heart, as much as Tyrel had become its voice.

"Maybe we can get some to defect." Thiba said, standing. "I'll push whoever we have space-side."

Always the one with the plan. And the brains to back them up. Tyrel already missed how she and Burly would argue. Like two heavyweights circling, testing each other with jabs and feints. Thiba would always win, of course.

She went into the hut, her terminal's glow the only light inside. Tyrel and Oto gazed into the bonfire, silhouettes flickering as survivors danced past the flames.

"Our spirits are stronger than we are." Oto muttered.

Tyrel nodded.

"But we're Tiānti's most valuable resource." He glanced toward the glittering bay. "Us, and the water."

Oto just grunted, unconvinced.

"Ty." Thiba poked her head through the hut's arched doorway. "You got a message."

He actually had two messages. The first was from Chaudhary: a request to meet. Neutral ground in Sheen. As if there was anything neutral on this planet, Tyrel thought. She would get her meeting, and then some.

The second was an update from the IMWA, this time from their CEO:

Dear Mr. Brand,

At the Interstellar Migrant Workers Alliance, we strive to lift up those whom the interstellar industrial complex has exploited. That's why we're always encouraged—and surprised—by stories like yours.

After tracking your descendants to Federated Oceania, it is my honor to inform you that we've located two surviving granddaughters. The eldest, Myra, is a clinician in Melbourne. We hope to arrange a meeting with her soon.

However, I'm reaching out personally because your situation presents a unique opportunity; both for yourself, and for the IMWA. Miraculously, your other granddaughter also resides in the Eridani system. Her employers have confirmed our findings. We've sent a contact request, including your information, through their channels.

Her name is Liya Chaudhary....

Tyrel sat, pondering that letter in the quiet darkness of Jiyu, long after the celebration had ended.

The day of the march, Tyrel didn't give a speech. He didn't need to: at dawn, thousands crammed the roads into Sheen. The first aurorae of spring faded above them, sky slipping from indigo to pastel.

Tyrel took his time, pulled by the slow tide of the crowd. He'd left Jiyu in the middle of the night, bundled up so he could sit on the hillside, looking at the stars. Thiba had pointed Sol out to him and Burly one night, however many months ago: a tiny dot, barely distinguishable from the rest.

Eighty-five years is a long time, Tyrel thought. But it was also a long way. Far enough to make his old home seem foreign—an infinitesimal speck, shrouded in memories that felt more and more like dreams. He knew they were both more and less than that. But time and distance—and the way they become the same thing as you get older—made a mirage of the sturdiest memories.

People patted Tyrel's back as they passed. They nodded,

smiled, got chants going. Their jumpsuits were patchworks of red and teal, blue and black, pieces stitched together and remade. No color or corporate logo could sort them now.

A few locals whizzed by on their bikes. Teenagers, thrilling the nearest survivors with their youth, their enthusiasm. Tyrel had a flash of Jordan out on the dunes, laughing as sand sprayed from his tires. Maybe, after all this, he'd go back to the Hallex archives. Try to catch whatever he could. The glimpses of his son he'd have to settle for.

As he reached Hazar, he saw the electric fences they'd put up around the farm towers, the Edict fabs, the Consortium cafeterias. A handful of security guards lingered behind the fences, looking miserable. Then Tyrel noticed the helmets littering the ground, the open gates where guards were shedding their armor and joining the march. Survivors embraced them, shaking their hands as they waved them on.

They kept moving, past the rec centers and bathhouses, into Sheen's industrial core. The chants grew louder as Tyrel approached the city center. The crowd knotted together. People held hands to keep from losing one another.

A cheer erupted up ahead. People pointed to the sky. A banner unfurled from the top floors of the Almani building, just as a passenger drone buzzed past. Fat blue letters read: WE ARE JAL.

The drone taxied above the rooftops, then descended over the Consortium headquarters, its stepped structure anchoring Sheen's streets. Tyrel jostled through the crowd, heart in his throat. That would be her, he thought. Flying in for their meeting.

Did she know? Would anything change if she did?

Word of Tyrel's arrival spread as he closed in on the Tiānti building. Rapt faces turned to see him. A path opened, clearing the way. Liberated workers reached out to brush his shoulders. Thousands of voices converged around those three words he'd said at Burly's funeral:

"We. Are. Jal."

"We. Are. Jal."

"We. Are. Jal."

Tyrel reached the end of the road. Featureless steel walls towered above him. A line of grim-faced security guards hid behind shields at the entrance gate. He waited, listening as the citywide refrain echoed through the streets. The chanting lapsed into wild cheers as the doors shuddered, then opened.

Chaudhary stepped out alone.

Liya Chaudhary. His granddaughter. Tyrel saw it now. The hints of Emi in her lighter features. The hints of Lexi. Of himself. An anthos-shaped pin glinted from her lapel.

Jal's native flower looked strange on her. A symbol of the resistance. Proof that life—real life, not the corporate slavery that Tiānti forced on them—could thrive on this inhospitable world. Tyrel never thought he'd see it on a Consortium suit.

But she wasn't just a suit. She was his kin. Like the people behind him. Like the security guards who'd joined the march. Like Oto. Like Thiba. Like Burly, the brother he never had.

Liya nodded, and the closest guards stood down, letting Tyrel through.

She held out her hand. Tyrel hesitated, fighting back tears as he saw the recognition reflected in her eyes. For the first time in nearly a century, Tyrel felt like he'd found his home.

It wasn't the sight of a long-lost relative that brought him home. Nor the half-forgotten cry of someone left behind. It wasn't the memories of what he'd missed, but the warmth of those around him.

Silence fell over the streets as Tyrel shook her hand. He glanced back, holding on as Liya tried to pull away. He saw the crowd's apprehension. Liya Chaudhary was the face of their oppressors. Tyrel understood that. He'd been there with them. Suffered with them. Grieved with them.

They'd endured so much. Swallowed so many empty promises. Could things really change? Could he really make their lives any better?

Tyrel turned to face the survivors. They needed a sign. Something to show them they were in this together, no matter the cost. He slipped his other hand around Liya's and raised their fists into the air, ears ringing as a triumphant cheer echoed across Jal.

Jeff Hewitt is a sci-fi writer living in Los Angeles. He grew up surrounded by water—in the swamps, lakes, and onion mucks of Upstate New York. He studied at Goldsmiths College. His work has appeared in *Slate*, *Escape Pod*, and *On Spec.*

Within the Seed Lives the Fruit

Leah Andelsmith

Morning dawns and Lou has exactly nothing left to give. She goes out to the garden anyway because that's the way she was taught, and she waters as the heavy hose drags behind her and threatens to knock down tomato plants or flatten the sweet potatoes. Between her tee shirt sleeves and leather work gloves are bare brown forearms and dark elbows. Her short Afro is salt and pepper all over, except at the temples, where it has begun to come in white. Her knees creak as she hefts the hose, and she stops for a moment to wipe sweat from her brow. That's when she notices the mint. The bindweed is wrapped around the stalk.

It has crept up in the night, or yesterday morning when her back was turned, or under the glaring noonday sun when everything else was too lethargic to grow. Stealthily it slid its tendrils up and around the stalk, opening its leaves and mingling them with the mint. It may seem like a dance, but the bindweed will choke the plant and drag it to the ground.

Lou puts down the hose and crouches low to get a closer look. Her heart sinks, seeing how tightly the bindweed is entwined, how hard it will be to untangle the vines. She lifts a mint leaf with her finger, already pale and soft where it should be bright green and strong. Lou feels heavy and tired. She wishes she could go back to the time when she hid her heart in the garden. She should pull out the small pair of scissors that are in her back pocket. She should slip off her work gloves and use her bare fingers to separate plant from weed, to save the former and kill the latter.

Instead, a bumblebee floats past and lands on the squash plant next to her. In no time, it is up to its abdomen in a yellow flower, wriggling and working, its thighs fat with pollen.

She sits back on her heels and looks at the green all around her, seeing the way the plants are unabashed in their abundance. Caressing the tip of the next post with a curling tendril. Reclaiming the paths by spreading across to touch a neighbor. Fanning out their broad leaves to shelter their fruit. Creating a shady interior.

The soft soil hidden under the mulch gives beneath her feet. The leaves rustle in the breeze. Even though she knows she's alone, Lou looks over each shoulder before laying face down. A bit clumsily, she shimmies so she can put her head between the stalks and peer through the leaves. More bees harvest pollen in this understory, buzzing softly as they fly from one bloom to the next. Lou wriggles further in, all the way to the center. She rests for a moment, catching her breath, not entirely sure why she wanted to crawl under.

Then, in the stillness, a young squash rolls an inch or two towards her as if pushed gently. It jingles, a muted chime coming from the pale green shell.

Lou suddenly remembers the sweet burst of juice from a warm, ripe cherry tomato, and a longing tears at her heart. She touches the squash and it jingles again.

Even though the part of her with the creaking knees says no, the work goes to waste if you pick the fruit unripe, Lou cuts the squash from its stem and hurries it to the kitchen.

"Louise? Louise is that you?" Lou's father Royal says from his armchair in the living room.

Lou doesn't answer. She takes out the cutting board and the knife.

"Did you get something from the garden? Let me weigh it."

Slice. A ring of light green flesh separates from the squash.

Royal—lanky, wiry, dressed in boots and overalls even though he doesn't work outside much anymore—enters the kitchen with slow and deliberate steps. "You don't even have the scale out," he says.

"Let me get it for you," he adds with a tired, patronizing tone, struggling to bend down to open the cupboard.

Slice. Each time she makes a cut, a soft chime comes from the squash.

"Will you stop? You have to weigh it first," he says, coming to stare over Lou's shoulder. "It's green! You picked it green?! Haven't I taught you . . . ."

Slice. Another thin portion comes off, and Lou sees a bit of brass through a translucent coating of flesh. She digs her fingers in, her nails filling with squash. She grasps the bell and pulls it out, a short length of string trailing from the brass loop at the top.

She can't quite breathe.

Jingle, jingle. She remembers sliding underneath a tomato plant.

Jingle, jingle. She remembers her eight-year old fingers scraping away enough dirt to make a cozy hollow for the bell.

Jingle, jingle. A gift she gave the garden, now given back to her.

"What is that bell, Louise?" Royal demanded, his voice getting sharper. "Is this some kind of joke?"

Lou shakes her head, staring down at the bell in her hands. "Yeah. It was a joke, Daddy. Ha, ha."

"That is not a funny joke. We can't waste food in this house! You know that." He's trying to be stern, but there's panic in his tone. His endless calculations. The price of the water and fertilizer for that squash wasted. The profit on the sale of it squandered.

Lou finally looks up at him, sees his worry, his fear, as if those men were knocking on the door right now. "It was a joke from Frankie down the road, Daddy. He gave me this squash. It didn't come from our garden."

Royal's shoulders slump as the tension leaves them. He bends down to put the scale away.

"Why didn't you just say so, Lou?" he says softly, touching her back. Then he shakes his head. "That damn fool Frankie. He never did get his head screwed on straight. Imagine wasting a perfectly good fruit like that."

Lou walks out to the porch, where she sits clutching the bell until nightfall.

The first year, before Lou was born, the mortgage for Royal and Marie's farm came through too late to plant. They finally had their land, but they wouldn't make a profit that year. Having seen other Black farmers tricked in this and all kinds of ways, Royal and Marie had saved up the first year's mortgage money along with the down payment and tucked it secretly away. They also found the bindweed, which would eat into their profits, and which neither the seller nor the bank had told them about.

Determined to grow something anyway that first year, they started a backyard garden with late season vegetables. Some people have green thumbs. Royal and Marie's hands were as brown as the soil, spreading richness and fertility wherever they worked. Royal weighed and measured it all, and Marie was a careful canner. They kept just enough to get them through the winter and sold the surplus. It was only a few bushels of collards, but they made a little bit of money.

They cultivated more and more acres of produce each year, but they kept that backyard garden, growing veggies in it that they didn't grow out in the rows. To eat from. To last them through the winter. To try out new seeds. Royal kept weighing each leaf and ear and fruit, calculating how much would go into canning jars, and later into a deep freezer for the winter.

Royal didn't spend money on luxuries and didn't want to be seen buying them. It was never smart to seem like you were doing too well for yourself, because someone would always punish you for getting ahead. But he made an exception one particularly abundant year, when they had made that year's payment and saved towards next year's payment too. Five candy canes for the kids, each with a bell tied around it, bought from a traveling peddler on his way out of town. The mint candy was cooling and burning at the same time, sharp and sweet. Lou let it dance and dissolve in her mouth. Ringing the bell, she was full of joy.

The following July, she crawled under a tomato plant, breathing in the herby scent of the foliage, stopping every few inches to eat the tomatoes on the lowest branches. They burst on her tongue, warm and sweet, tangy and savory at once. She buried her jingle bell there next to the main stalk, all the way at the center.

The summer after that, a little horse figurine washed up in the ditch along the road. She shouldn't have touched it; if it was another child's, she might have been accused of stealing. But its coat was a beautiful brown, with red undertones, like the living soil itself, and she shoved it into the pocket of her dress before anyone could see her take it. If no one knew about it, she could have something special and not have to share it with her brothers and sisters.

Instead she shared the figurine with the one soul that understood her. The paths in the garden were marked with stones. She started at the corner of the squash patch and counted one, two, three, four, five, turned over that stone and made a depression big enough for the tiny horse. She pictured it in its bed of soil, as safe under its rock as she was tucked in her sheets.

A year later, the bindweed stole one of her buttons. Reached out and pulled it right off her dress. She didn't see the tendrils curling around the white button as she pressed up against a tomato plant, carefully unwinding and unwrapping that very bindweed from it. She was ten, with newly nimble fingers and an improved attention span, and Royal had entrusted her with this delicate task for the first time.

She didn't know the bindweed stole her button and was never able to figure out how it came off her dress, much less explain it to her mama. But since she was being a good helper, she didn't get in much trouble for losing it. Later Marie had even let her select its replacement from the button box. Lou chose one that was bright green and shiny. It didn't match the other buttons, which were small and white against the fading pink plaid of her cotton dress, but it reminded her of juicy cucumbers and zucchini.

Lou's younger siblings avoided the garden, but she spent as much time in it as possible. She sought the secret low places that her parents were too big and busy to crawl under. The garden wasn't work yet then; it was still magic, and Lou still knew how to see the world from its underside. She would lay on her belly under the squash plants, not caring about the prickly stems, and the leaves would fan out above her like parasols. She found caterpillars there, and bindweed silently spreading. Tender green leaves shaped like arrowheads sprouted from a thin vine that wound its way around the squash stems like a garrote.

"Louise," her father would say, "Pull those weeds, like I told you." Perspiration on his dark brown forehead would run like stormwater through the deep creases he made by frowning in the sun as he worked. He used a kerchief to mop the salty sweat and keep it from stinging his eyes. He was never happy until he'd weighed the tomatoes, counted the ears of corn, calculated the return on the money he'd spent on seeds and fertilizer.

Lou would lay in the undersides, where the smell of the soil was close. The mineral scent of rock and sand and clay that had been there since the beginning of time. The fungal funk of tiny bodies, vibrant and alive, working the soil from life to death to life again; of insects grazing on organic material and shredding it to bits; of fungi and bacteria hugging plants' roots and passing them the nutrients they needed to survive. The damp and fragrant decay of every leaf and stem and stalk that had ever perished there, which contained the promise of every seedling that had yet to sprout and flourish. She would close her eyes and breathe and breathe and breathe, drawing in the scent of all her yesterdays and tomorrows. She felt rich then.

"Pull the weeds, Louise," Royal would say to her feet sticking out from underneath the leaves. "Cut the stem right at the ground." But often, she would keep her scissors closed beside her and touch the bindweed's soft leaves as gently as she could, studying their streamlined shape, watching as they gave just so beneath her finger. "It doesn't matter what I do," Lou thought at those times. "The bindweed always comes back."

When she was twelve, she snuck the white pawn from the chess set in the family room. She had won for the first time against her father, gotten her first hint at how it might feel to be grown up. She pushed the piece into the garden soil with the tip of her finger, her face inches away, watching as grains of earth fell in on the rounded top, wanting it to be saved and protected forever.

She didn't say anything when the piece turned up missing, even helped to look below the furniture and in all the drawers. Royal cut a one-inch slice from the narrow end of a corn cob and squared it off. He let it dry out on the window sill, and they played with that as one of the pawns. Lou loved how the feather-dry piece barely grazed her hand, so light it was liable to blow away.

Marie died soon after that, giving birth to her sixth baby. Royal turned to Lou as the oldest child to be the trustworthy one. To be the hardest worker. To be careful with the placement of every seed, the harvest of each and every fruit. Marie had taken in washing to supplement what they made off of their crops, and they couldn't make it without that money, so Royal started doing odd jobs—making deliveries, cutting wood, and entrusting more of the farm work to Lou.

Lou put away the magic of the garden the same way she tucked away her grief, protecting all the sharp and delicate corners, swaddling it in warm blankets and old clothes, out of sight. There were no more bells and buttons for the garden. Her gifts were well-cured compost and hose water on hot days.

"The garden can't be magic anymore, Louise," she told herself. "You have to help Daddy. Don't say, 'because Mama isn't here.' Just pretend she's always been gone. Don't say, 'no more time to be in the undersides.' Just go out and harvest and pull the weeds. You have to, because we can't lose the land."

Royal had had a hard enough time getting the mortgage to begin with, and they would snatch the farm from the family in a second if they could. Sometimes the white men came with guns in the dark, and sometimes they came with paperwork in the daylight. The law said one thing about equal treatment, but Royal and Lou had seen Black farmer after Black farmer lose their land. Several cousins. Three neighbors.

So Lou's father had rules. Every item of produce weighed and recorded to make sure they would be on track that year. No fruit wasted, not a single one, lest that dime be the difference between a full mortgage payment and a short one. Work extra and save every penny for the bad years. Never seem like you're getting on too poorly, or too well. Keep your head down and stay out of trouble in town. Royal would never have spoken up himself, but it was known among the young freedom fighters that they could get a plate at the back porch after dark, or even sleep warm and covered in the hayloft if they stayed quiet.

Lou came to know it as deeply as Royal did. One payment late or short and they'd take the farm. One step out of line, one petition signed or protest meeting attended, and they would come for you. You sell your produce, pay your mortgage, make your taxes. Live your life walking a tightrope, and maybe you'll get to keep what you have.

One thing her father learned was to make a will. As a child, Royal's best friends were two brothers living down the road on their family's homeplace. The orchards and fields and woods and farmhouse had belonged to the whole family equally, but some real estate investment firm got a distant cousin to sell his share of the land. When the company came to collect, the court put the land up for sale. The family didn't have the cash to buy it back, but a timber company did.

Better for one person to have it all, to keep it and take care of it, than to split it among scattered children and grandchildren who moved away to the city. Royal didn't trust the courts any more than his neighbors, but sometimes playing a rigged game is less dangerous than not playing at all.

While Lou stayed and planted seeds and cared for the soil, her younger siblings sprouted and grew up and walked right off the farm. Their lives had grown fat like tomatoes, especially that Francine, who worked in a fancy bank and wore high heels every day. But Royal wanted to make his land stick, so the children that moved away got nothing.

Lou grew up too, but she never left the life she knew and the garden she loved. Someone had to be there for their father who had given them everything. Someone had to make sure they didn't lose the farm. And so, Lou learned to pick the bindweed. She looked sharply for those tiny arrowhead leaves wrapped around a stalk, untwined it with delicate fingers and snipped it away with a small, sharp pair of scissors.

"We'll never get rid of this bindweed completely, Louise," Royal would say. "But if we catch it in time, we can save the plant. And if we keep after it hard enough, we might manage to keep it out of the fields."

Every day she watched her father pour his love deep into the land as if replenishing the groundwater. Most farmers would till the soil, but Lou and Royal left it alone, only turning what they had to in order to plant. Royal never left any soil uncovered, couldn't bear to do it any more than he would have let one of his children go without clothing. When there was nothing left to plant, Lou dug her hand into the sack of clover seed they kept dry in the corner of the root cellar.

And the family did hold on to the farm, despite the odds. Once the mortgage was paid off, Lou convinced Royal to let her take on the odd jobs instead. She took on more and more of the farm work too, and took the produce to sell at farmers markets, until she was doing it all herself. Giving and giving. Until her knees began to creak and her back began to ache. And still giving more.

They kept playing chess through the years, sitting down for a game a few times each winter, sometimes Lou winning, sometimes Royal. At some point, Lou started winning every single game. Royal would hoard his pieces and keep them to the back, even forfeiting turns instead of moving a piece he didn't want to. Or else he would put the king out in front of the other pieces and try to use it to fight.

All these years you played a slow and careful game and you won, Lou wanted to tell him. It's okay to let go a little. We're all fine. Eventually, she slipped the game to the furthest corner of the closet and they didn't play anymore.

Though she said she would stop after her mother died, Lou did entrust something else to the garden's safekeeping, one last time when she was a teenager. Lou's favorite cousin, who had grown up right here, right down the road, came back to visit. The kids gathered near the honeysuckle, surrounded by its perfume, picking blossoms and sucking out the sweet, floral nectar just like the bees. The cousin told stories of a world beyond the farm, beyond their town. Places that Lou knew about from books and school but could only dream of visiting.

Cities where more money was spent in a day than her town would see in a decade. Every day walking past hundreds of people you had never seen before and would never see again.

An ocean so big you couldn't see the end of it. Churning water that felt peaceful. Waves and sand that wore down broken bottles.

The cousin had a piece of sea glass for each of them. Lou's fingers whispered over the surface her piece, taking in the shape of its curves. To turn something sharp and painful into something smooth and soft and comforting in its beauty seemed to her an impossibility. The family survived by knowing that sharp meant sharp, and you'd better not touch or you'd get hurt. Don't reach, don't talk or dream out of turn. Don't call attention to yourself, don't make waves.

Her cousin promised them there were other options, but Lou still didn't think she wanted to leave her family's land. She'd have to risk losing something she knew she loved, just to find out whether or not there was something better. That didn't feel like freedom to her. But the dream of strangers and ocean waves was precious, so she planted it in the garden, hoping one day it would bear fruit.

Night falls and Lou is still sitting on the porch. The planks beneath her are soft from years of footfall and warm from the day's sunlight.

She traces the raised grain of the wood with her fingertips and tells herself again that this small porch and all the rest of the farm are truly theirs now, and have been for some time. With some trepidation, she tries to let her heart settle into that knowledge. Not reminding her father of the fact, but knowing it within herself and believing it. It's like dipping her toe into a deliciously warm bath. Her bones ache to slip all the way in, but she's scared to let go.

She rolls the jingle bell between fingers and palm, listening to the tiny ball within as it tries to ring out against the muted sides. Every now and then she holds it by the string and shakes it, letting the chimes mix with the starlight.

Jingle, jingle. What now? the bell seems to say. *Jingle, jingle. There's joy for you too, Lou.*

The next day, she is picking green peppers and one of them rattles. She drops the basket right there, takes the pepper in her palms and presses her thumbs into the flesh until they burst through with a juicy snap. Flecks of vivid green speckle her shirt, and a bright, vegetal scent fills her nose as she tears the pepper open. Inside is a white chess pawn. Lou brings it into the house, puts it back in the crumbling paperboard box in the back corner of the closet and slips the airy piece of corn cob into her pocket. It makes her feel so light, she doesn't notice as a sprig of bindweed stuck to her shoe takes the opportunity to stay behind in the closet.

She lies on her side one day, mesmerized by a tiny horse galloping in circles on the leaf of a cucumber plant, trampling yellow and black-spotted cucumber beetles with its hooves. Heart ready to burst, breath caught in her throat. She stays still, still, still as delight spreads over her skin.

The wind rustling in green leaves begins to whisper through Lou's open window as she drifts off at night. She dreams of the brown, yellow and red earth underneath the garden plants, and she smells the minerals and living decay as she sleeps. Waking, Lou sends her thoughts down into that soil like roots.

When the corn comes ripe, one ear has kernels made of golden glass, shining with the sun underneath its frosted surface. "Did I miss out by staying put?" she asks herself, the glass ear real and heavy in her hand. "Maybe not," she answers. "Maybe some people don't have to travel the world to be free."

The next morning, Lou skips breakfast and sets off for town

immediately after watering. The lawyers are coming to the library to do their pro bono work today, and she gets a spot near the front of the line. She has to make sure the farm goes to someone who will keep it and care for it.

When she comes back hours later, Royal is trying to drag the hose from the side of the house to the garden, his brows pressed down tight over his eyes in concentration. He jerks and jerks with one hand, trying to keep hold of the porch railing with the other, his legs spindly beneath him.

Lou begins to trot and then to run, the brim of her straw hat catching the air and flying off onto the dusty road. She reaches him just as he gives one last wild flail, losing hold of the hose and flying backwards. She can't stop him from falling, but she gets her hands behind his head and cushions it from cracking against the stair, keeping hold of him even as her back explodes in pain.

His skin is hot and dry, not a drop of sweat despite the brilliant noon sun. His face is twisted in confusion, his eyes unable to focus on Lou as she leans over him.

"Someone has to take care of that garden," he says. Lou shakes her head, a lump rising up in her throat. She swallows it down.

"I know, Daddy, but we don't water at noon, remember? I watered this morning, and I'll go out again later."

"Someone has to—" He tries to get up, but fades immediately.

"Shh, it's alright. The garden is fine. The tomatoes are perfect this year. Everyone is fine," she says. "Let's go upstairs."

She scoops her arm below his shoulders, pulling him up as he gets his feet beneath him. He is as thin as a beanstalk, as light as an okra seed.

It's an effort to get upstairs. Lou doesn't know if she's dripping sweat or tears, doesn't know if she's crying from the pain in her back or the drying leaf that has been substituted for her father's body.

She helps him into the bed, where he recovers from the heat stroke, but never regains his strength. In moments of delirium he tries to get up, asks her question after question.

"Did you water?"

"Yes, Daddy, I did."

"Did you count the ears of corn?"

"Yes, Daddy, you can rest now."

He puts his hand on her shoulder, fixes her eyes with a

desperate strength that seems like clarity. "Are we going to make our payment this year? Is there going to be enough?"

"We paid off the mortgage thirty years ago. Do you remember? We went to the bank."

Lou remembers. She remembers the tears in his eyes, clutching his hat in his hands, so happy he didn't quite know what to do. But also lost because he didn't quite know what to do. A man in his early sixties, Royal's whole life had been making that mortgage payment. He kept asking the loan officer if that was all, if it was really done.

"Daddy, the mortgage is paid. We're all going to be fine now. It's okay to rest," Lou says. Sometimes it's enough to calm him, and sometimes he worries himself to sleep.

In the weeks since it arrived, the unnoticed sprig of bindweed has tentatively sent out a tiny root tip, seeking the dusty, dirty spaces between the floorboards and feeding on the nutrients in the wood. Its roots have also found a thin pipe and worked their delicate, forceful way through the weak spots to touch the cool water inside.

Now this garden astronaut sends out a shoot from its top, along with a paper-thin leaf of the softest green. The bindweed works its way up and up, climbing the walls, anchoring in door jambs and cracks in the plaster, up to the second floor bedroom of one who is both adversary and friend.

Now that Royal can't go out anymore, it is the bindweed that cares enough to come to him. Royal has been the life of the garden as much as the leaves and the roots and the soil. For years he worked his love through every stem and blossom. And so the bindweed sees him like it does any other plant: as part of itself.

One morning Royal does not wake. A single vine of bindweed is wrapped around his wrist, bright green and healthy. Though it is too late, Lou gets the scissors anyway and carefully cuts it away.

Lou remembers being a child in the undersides, close to the bindweed. She knew the squash would die if she didn't pull the bindweed away, but she also knew that the bindweed was hungry too. Maybe she was as prepared for this at ten as she is now.

She clutches her Christmas bell.

Jingle, jingle. Like when we slice a head of cabbage from its stem.

Jingle, jingle. Like when the corn dies back in the fall.

Jingle, jingle. Like when we pull up a pepper plant that the bindweed got.

Lou's siblings come back for the funeral. They bury Royal next to Marie, in the family plot way out in the corner of the open field by the trees. His will states, "To my dearest Lou, I leave my land. She has loved it as I have."

Lou's whole life has been keeping hold of the land he bought. Now she's in her late sixties, the land is hers, and she doesn't quite know what to do. Francine and the others sit next to her, hold her hand, offer to let her stay at their places in the city. They mean well, but they don't really understand.

The day after her siblings leave, Lou finds her white button. She chips a tooth on it in one of the largest okras and spits it clattering back onto the plate. The plain cotton threads from her childhood dress have been replaced with a fine golden cord running a ring through the two holes.

The pink plaid dress is long gone, but the green button is still in the button box. When she handed the dress down, it was cut off and replaced with one that matched better, for the sister who didn't want to be teased.

A sharp pain shoots from Lou's hips to her knees as she rises from the table. She hasn't been able to stand up fully straight since catching her father. Lou returns the white button to the button box and pulls out the green one that she has treasured all these years. With a few quick stitches, she attaches it to her shirt front like a brooch.

Putting her button back on makes her feel more like herself than she has since her mother died more than five decades ago. "All these years, all this work, it hasn't only been for Daddy. It's been for the garden itself, too," she says to herself. "But if I could have it my way, I'd just as soon go back to how it was when I was little. There's no need to pack this grief away like I did with Mama."

Lou leaves five letters in the mailbox for the postman to pick up, so her siblings will know she's gone and not coming back. Then she returns at last to her dearest friend.

The garden is a green jewel in the sunlight. The zucchini have grown to the size of her forearms. The tomatoes are bursting on the vine. The bees float on the sun-thick air, their thighs still fat with pollen. Like she has always done, she will give the garden herself. Her back aches anyway, and she would like to lie down.

She crawls underneath the leaves. The soft soil of the garden fills in every curve and bend of her spine, rising to meet her. It's like slipping into a hot bath.

She waits there as the bindweed takes over the squash plants, as high summer passes into September. She breathes in the green and the damp of the soil. The earth and plants cover over her body. Roots nestle in her upturned palm. Her flesh shrivels like a raisin. Her body shrinks down to something like an insect's egg.

Lou's siblings clear the house and carry out her will. The garden browns and the frost comes while Lou remains, a tiny seed in the soil, hibernating. Incubating.

The frosts subside and the new folks begin to plant. Lou is now amongst the overwintering carrots with her feet down beneath her and the very crown of her head poking above the ground. But she doesn't wait to be harvested. As soon as the ground warms, she stretches her arms and legs into the soil around her, her fingernails filling with dirt. She pulls herself up and out, her tiny body warming in the early spring sun.

She looks different now, just as the seed looks different from the plant, the plant looks different from the flower, and the flower looks different from the fruit. Her skin is the exact red-brown of the soil and her deep brown eyes shine with a joyful knowing. Her hair is a crown of coils in grey and silver and bright white nestling around her horns, which start behind her ears and spiral back to tapered points, like two feathers in a cap. Her knees are as resilient as they were when she was eight, and her bare feet are cushioned by tough callouses. Her clothes are the brown of dead leaves. In her pocket is a tiny bell, and right in the middle of her shirtfront is a single bright green button the size of a match head, sparkling as it catches the morning light.

"Francine can eat her heart out," she says, and also, "There's magic to be done."

She carves out a burrow for herself in the soil of the garden. Then she visits the newly sprouted seedlings, which reach up to her waist. By day she cups their tender green leaves in her hands and whispers to them. By night she tickles their roots so that they grow out happy and strong. On cloudy days, she touches each leaf with the light in her eyes. When the weather is too dry, she sprinkles tiny handfuls of water near their stalks.

When the plants grow tall, she moves house, camping high in the corn where the stalks meet the growing ears, folding the leaves down around her like tent flaps. She cuts through the skins of cherry tomatoes with sharp pebbles to scoop out the pulp and reaches into squash flowers to get at the nectar, her arms emerging fat with pollen. She picks aphid eggs off the backs of leaves and bursts them between her teeth, relishing the salty, meaty pop. She puts her entire face into kernels of corn, devouring the sweet, sticky flesh.

The bindweed vines are as thick as saplings to her now. She breaks off a sliver of an abandoned snail shell and runs the edge against a rock until it is as sharp as a scythe. She crops the vines to tiny stumps at ground level, then climbs up like a logger in a tree, sawing off chunks of vine to free the plants.

"You never learned how to love, did you?" she asks the bindweed. "You're just as tender as the plants you live on, and you need this garden just as much as you destroy it."

She knows that the broken roots of bindweed can sprout new vines, and these she seeks out while they are tiny, stomping them back into the ground. That she still has to do this work doesn't surprise her, not really. Without the struggle, there is no life. And without life, there is no joy.

In the high heat of summer, she digs a cave into an eggplant growing close to the stalk, forgotten and left to grow gargantuan. The spongy flesh is cool and not too humid, with an astringent scent. The seeds have a tender, nutty crunch, laced through with bitterness. The plumpest ones she saves in her pockets for planting next spring.

Lou watches the girl from the house walk up and down the paths, touching each leaf and flower, pressing her face against the foliage when she thinks no one is looking. The girl turns over tomato leaves, pats the white aphid eggs clustered beneath as lightly as her fingers will allow, then turns the leaves back over again without killing a single one.

Lou chose the new family because she wanted to keep the land in Black hands, and because she knows these folks have more than she and her father did. They have college degrees, and they know how to solicit donations and apply for grants. They have a team to help with the work, not just the one family. They have a plan to feed the community. And now they have the land. Outright. They won't have to live looking over their shoulder.

When the girl begins to leave small gifts in the garden, Lou holds on to them. The friendship bracelet she made at camp. A single silver earring, shaped like a teardrop. Love letters on loose leaf paper, written and folded and never delivered.

When the grown-ups start leaving gifts, Lou receives those as well. A golden dollar from their first produce sale that spring. Heaped teaspoons of braised collard greens that fill her nose with the sharp scent of vinegar and make her mouth water. Thimbles of strawberry wine, crisp and honeyed on her tongue. Finger-sized loaves of cornbread so freshly-baked that steam wafts out earthy and sweet when Lou breaks them open. Although the new folks don't ever see her, they sense that there is another pair of brown hands spreading richness and fertility, working the land alongside them.

Lou keeps what the bindweed steals, too. A sticker once worn proudly on a shirt. A lucky penny, lifted out of a pocket. A necklace, its fragile chain broken.

When the garden starts to yellow and brown, Lou returns to her burrow, nibbling on the starchy roots of the dying plants. Using her snail-shell scythe like a pick, she hollows out niches along the earthen walls, carefully placing in them the colorful bracelet curled into a spiral, the love letters lined up like family albums on a shelf, the shiny golden dollar like a little sun, the earring dripping like water. Though she knows they are only borrowed, she cherishes each present, keeping them safe, waiting for the right moment to give them back. The bindweed's items have their own place in the dark corners at the end of her burrow, where the open space narrows and rejoins the earth. She'll help the bindweed give those back too, whenever the green garrote decides it's time.

Leah Andelsmith is a Black, queer afro-futurist and fantasy writer. Her fiction has appeared in *midnight & indigo* and *FIYAH*, and her creative nonfiction has appeared in the *Arts Paper* in New Haven. She enjoys visiting her favorite trees on neighborhood walks, staying at the museum all day, and keeping library books well past their due date. You can find her at leahandelsmith.com

Shelton Johnson Calls

Amuri Morris

Amuri Morris is an artist based in Richmond, VA. She recently graduated from Virginia Commonwealth University with a degree in painting/printmaking and business. She has acquired several artistic accolades including a VMFA fellowship. She aims to promote diversity in art canon, specifically focusing on the black experience. You can find her work at www.murisart.com or on instagram under @miss.muri.art.

One With the Ground

Guillermo G. Mendoza

I prayed a manda, you know? Before the necklace, before everything. I asked la Virgencita for help with Abuelito's land, and I offered to act as her in the Via Crucis procession. But I got to be Jesus. Kinda.

That day Mamá didn't wanna leave me alone with the company's trocas roaming town. Not after the threat. She thought of calling her boss at the maquila and asking for a couple days off, but she went in the end. "I'll be fine, Mami, don't worry," I told her at the bus stop, pale sunrise above us. We kissed each other goodbye like any other day. No idea we'd never meet again. At least not in person, because next Sunday she didn't come back. They asked her to work extra over the weekend. She returned after it was all over.

I drank a couple cups of coffee for breakfast. I needed them. The trucks rattled over the dirt track around the house all night long. They did that on purpose, to snatch away our sleep. To wear us down so we'd sell them Abuelito's land. But we wouldn't. Soon they left anyway, so I put on your Cruz Azul hoodie and got to work. I'd used it since you left. It reminded me you were in el norte, looking after us. It smelled of you at first, but that soon faded off. Still, I wore it to feel you close, and that day I needed you with me.

I cleaned Abuelito's room, and that's when I found it. I'd put it off for weeks because I always wept as soon as I walked in. Couldn't take he was gone. But you were about to come back to help us with the lawsuit, and where would you and Norma and Juanito sleep? So I cleaned the mess up and swept and mopped, flooded in tears. Every sway chlorinated my heart, washed away my grief. I took his things one by one, caressed them. And I found it, below a pile of crumbing pics: Abuela Tonantzin's necklace, a small Tree of Life shaped out of clay. You must remember it: She wears it in every photo, around her neck. I held it, palm open. Its weight was like a mountain. It kinda felt alive in my hand, like I held a lizard or something. Took a pic of it and texted Ma: "Look what sprung up!" I expected a voicemail, an old anecdote for an answer, but you know . . . . They don't want her on the phone while at work. She texted back next day: "Mamá

Tona's necklace.... It's an amulet, mija. Keep it. It will protect you." And I did. Everything else we gave away to the parish.

I went back to church after school. The parish managed to get a drama teacher to come from the city in the afternoons, to help the youth group mount the Via Crucis' procession. I'd signed up, so I walked through the atrium, past the teocotes' dancing shade, all the way to the utility room in the back. I could see them through the window warming up already, so I hurried.

The teacher set a new challenge: to improvise a scene with stuff we had in our pocket. No dialogue, no partner, just me and whatever I carried. And all I had was the necklace. So when my turn came I stepped forward. The teacher applauded: my time was on. I held the Tree of Life in my hands as if it was a wounded bird. She clapped again, and the drama crew too. The bird became a baby—your son Juanito, my little nephew. I cuddled him, took him to my breast and sang a lullaby. Another round of applause. I found myself swaying abuelito's ashes, eyes wet. They cheered one last time. His ashes became a ceiba seed. I kneeled and planted it on the ground. I watered it with with my tears. Then I rose with closed eyes, unfolding my arms towards the ceiling, and pictured in my mind a tree rushing out of the seed.

And it did. The ceiba snapped into the room. Like a dream, only it wasn't. The teacher and the drama crew saw it too. The world stilled, a silence. Then flickers of awe. A few went to their knees and prayed. Word spread right away.

All night I looked for an explanation. I even went back next morning before school, to see if all that about a tree sprouting out my imagination was real. Guess what? It was still there, tiles broken by the roots, branches so high they reached the ceiling, surrounded by a crowd of rezanderas who murmured and counted beads in their rosaries. It was fully grown, bark like a lizard's skin roughed and thorned, branches hanging low like arms extended towards the praying women. And hung in one of the lower branches, as if the ceiba rose it from the ground, Abuela Tonantzin's necklace. With all the rush, I'd left it behind the day before. I wonder how no one else found it. Anyway I took it back.

"Cipactli, what are your thoughts on this?"

It was the Social Studies teacher, the same one you took class with. You know him: Che Guevara shirts every single day, zapatista cap he never takes off. I snapped out of my daydream.

"Que qué teacher?"

"What do you think about the ejidos expropriation in 1990? San Miguel Ototipac lost half its common land so the state government could build the capital's beltway. I was just talking about it."

The teacher always liked talking politics with tangled words. And I knew the kind of answers he liked to hear. You know I was always good with words. Always the one asked to recite poems on Mother's Day, to pledge allegiance to the flag out loud for the whole school to follow. But that morning I couldn't deliver. My tongue knit into a hank and all I could do was stare out the window, beyond the soccer court and the cornfields, towards Abuelo Juan's plot.

The teacher waited.

I spat out:

"That it sucked."

I don't know why I then took my hand to abuela Tonantzin's necklace and knew what to do.

I went straight to don Ramiro's wasteland when class was over. It was dry from years of chemical fertilizers. It was the perfect place to try. I set the necklace on the ground, closed my eyes, and imagined a garden growing. When I opened them it was like one of those documentaries the biology teacher used to play, remember? Like one of those scenes where you can see months go by in few seconds.

A grove sprouted in the dead land. And when I picked the necklace up, it didn't vanish either.

Don Ramiro went crazy. He went to church to thank la Virgencita for the miracle, he even turned down his land's sale. The company even sent its 'security personnel' after him, to 'negotiate.' But by then the ceiba was the hottest news, and when the news broke about his wasteland turned to grove overnight, the whole town went crazy too. So everyone was at the church, even people from nearby towns. The padre came from the city even though it wasn't Sunday, just to see if what he'd heard on the phone was true. There was such a big crowd in town that nobody feared the company's thugs, despite them showing off their guns. Rumor went around about building a chapel at don Ramiro's and asking the bishop to come declare it holy ground. The miracles of the ceiba and don Ramiro's land were all you could hear.

But in the meanwhile, there was something else going on at Abuelo Juan's: they'd finished the wall and raised a signboard saying, "Gaia's Grove: Your Own Ecological Paradise." They'd already flattened it to build. So I went there that very night. Had to dodge the trucks, but in the end I snuck in.

You would've cried too. Remember the cazahuite tree in the corner, where the swallows nested? And the medlar we climbed as kids? Gone. All of it was. El tecorral where the lizards sunbathed, the knoll the mushrooms crawled over after it rained, the shack where the cacomixtles hid... all gone. An eerie extent of flattened sand was all their ghastly lamps displayed. And the concrete wall, all around. Abuelo Juan's beloved terreno split up into lots, ready to be built upon.

I looked towards the guard's cabin: the window flashed blue. He had the TV on. I walked to the middle of the plot, put the necklace on the ground, and let my imagination fly.

Saplings came out of the ground.

We didn't meet Abuelita Tonantzin, you and I. We just had family pics to know her by. So I always asked Abuelo Juan about her. "Abuelito, how was she like?"

"She was a very wise woman, mijita, very good with plants," he'd say first, and then carry on about her life. That's how I know who she was, what she did. She helped pretty much everyone in town when in childbirth. She healed those in need. Just for the sake of helping them, never a charge, all with herbs, stones and prayer, like una curandera from legend.

Abuelito really missed her. I felt it in his voice every time he talked about her. But he never got sad, al revés: joy sprang in him. One day I asked him why. "Es que she's still right here, with me, with us, mija. She never leaves." We were in his terreno, foraging mushrooms, and I thought he meant it as a metaphor or something. Pero no.

The real estate company brought back the machines to clear the copse of trees grown overnight. Meanwhile, people crowded outside the wall; it was the third 'miracle' in less than a week. The night guard swore he'd seen it all: vegetation grew out of nowhere, trees reached heights of decades in seconds, long gone herbs from the time of our abuelas sprouted por montones, buds exploded into flowers like fireworks made of petals. He told it all, then resigned and left for Juquila in pilgrimage. I still don't know how he didn't see me standing there in the middle of everything. But only the guys from drama knew who did the magic, the miracle or whatever. Oh, some of them talked all right. About the girl with the Tree of Life amulet. But nobody heard them. I guess people chose to believe in la Virgencita.

Didn't matter at first. The company flattened it all again. They were eager to build, because that proved they owned our land already despite the lawsuit. But I would use the necklace again. I'd perform its magic, because the land was our abuelitos' and they were trying to take it from us. Like they'd done before with other families, and even with the community ejidos on the slopes of the hill. Back then, not long ago really, they leveraged our poverty and misunderstandings and took advantage of the government's corrupción to change the land use permit. Then they crammed our town with armed men in trocas and also harnessed our fear. And now Abuelo Juan was gone, and they tried to steal his land from us. Su tierra which he cared for all his life. But I wouldn't let them.

So I went back that night. People were camped outside the plot's main gate already, Guadalupanos trying to witness the miracle. I went around them and followed the wall, looking for a spot dark enough to jump out of sight. And I found it, right in a corner. An ahuehuete grew tall next to the creek, and its shade made the wall pitch black. It was like they read my mind, the guys from drama: they were there, waiting for me in the dark. With their help, everything was easier, and soon we were inside. The new guard must've been in the toilet or something, because he was nowhere around. So I set the necklace on the land once again, in the middle of the plot, and I imagined something vaster than before.

And a thick wood emerged.

I was late for school the next day. One of the real estate company's trocas camped outside our home after sunrise. I thought they wouldn't dare to break in, not with the whole town roused by the miracles. Still, I waited long after they were gone. When I went out, I saw the message scratched over the gate, saying they would fuck me up if I didn't stop. I tried to calm myself down. "They won't do it, Cipactli, they wouldn't," I kept telling myself. But my body shook all the way to school, and any rattle of a wheel over the dirt made me jump out of the road and hide.

I went back anyway. That night and the next and the next. Their threats didn't stop, pero neither did I. I couldn't stop and leave our abuelito's land for them to snatch. And they already knew it was me, así que I just slept over at the parish for safety. It stood open now twenty four hours, as pilgrims arrived from neighboring towns for a chance to watch the miracle. The real estate company brought more and more men and guns to keep the crowd outside the wall. Jumping over it got harder, but the drama crew kept showing up, and every time we managed to get in unseen. Each dawn, thick woods covered the plot. And by night it was chopped down again.

I started falling asleep in class. I wouldn't last much longer, but I thought the company had to give up soon, because the bishop declared Abuelo's terreno holy ground a couple days after it all began. Some parishioners were even at the capital, lobbying for the realtor to give it back to the community. They wanted to build a sanctuary for la Virgencita there. But there was also the money: how much had the company spent already? They couldn't rent all those dozers and steamrollers much longer. They had to step back, someday. Those were my thoughts that last time, as I climbed over the wall with the help of a couple guys from drama.

I jumped over and looked at the guard's cabin. He was nowhere to be seen. Outside the wall, no prayers were sung, no murmurs sounded like the nights before. Somehow I didn't find that odd. I walked towards the center of the plot, under the ghastly light of the lamps. I put the necklace on the ground, then heard the shouts from my companions. Warnings. All too late: something pierced my back.

I didn't know where I was. I felt neither cold nor hot. All was dark. Something pressed on me from everywhere, and I couldn't move. Or rather, I had no body to move. It went on like that for who knows how long. Then the whispers came. Like rustling sounds, like the hissing of a snake, they called me: "Cipactli . . . Ci . . . pac . . . tli . . . " And somehow, I recognized them. The whispered voices belonged to the medlar, the cazahuite, the teocotes torn apart by the dozers. They were the mushrooms' underground nerves no longer growing, the gophers and worms and lizards buried alive in their furrows by the steamrollers. "Ci . . . pac . . . tli," they whispered in entangled voices. After a while I recognized the human ones among them: nuestras ancestras, elder women, called me. "Cipactli . . . Ci . . . pac . . . tli."

The other guys from drama managed to escape. Me, they left right here in the ditch. The necklace broke in my fist, but I no longer needed it. The voices and I raised the forest night after night. Every morning, there it was: enorme, frondoso. The men running the real estate company chopped it down every time, until we won. They never could never understand what happened. Just like they couldn't explain what my remains were doing in the plot.

The drama crew told the convenient version of the story, made it true by repetition: we broke into the plot to watch the miracle. The armed men were there. They grabbed the guys, molested me. I defended myself and got beaten down. My friends struggled to protect me. Shots got fired. They managed to escape; I didn't. And no one saw me again. The company couldn't prove its innocence. What were they gonna say? That a bruja grew a forest over their stolen plot every night?

El pueblo went mad. The whole town camped around the terreno and painted slogans on the wall. They occupied the city hall and closed down the highways. They marched to the capital and took over the real estate company CEO's office. It all reached national news, and the federal government had to step in. That's how they found what was left of my human body. But you already saw that, hermano. You were back, and you saw how the company left for good.

The only thing I regret is leaving like that, without saying adiós to Mamá. Identifying my corpse broke her heart. I wish I could tell her I'm not really gone, que estoy aquí. I wish you could hear me whenever you come here, to abuelo Juan's land. But I know you feel my love in the flowers' scent, in the embracing moisture of the ground and the cool shade of the trees. It is all for you. I like it when you play above me with Juanito, mi sobrinito. I like to hear you all laugh. Still, I wish you could hear me, hermano, like you did when we were kids and I told you bedtime stories. I wish I had my voice again, to speak with human words, to whisper in your ear, "Oye, I'm not gone, they didn't kill me, hermanito, not really." To tell you I live in every patch of this land Abuelo Juan tilled with so much love. To tell you that, like Abuela Tonantzin and the women before her, I became one with the ground.

Una con el suelo

Guillermo G. Mendoza

Hice una manda, ¿sabes?, antes del collar, antes de todo. Le pedí a la Virgencita que nos ayudara con lo del terreno y yo la representaría en el Viacrucis. Pero me tocó ser Jesús. O algo así.

Ese día mamá no quería dejarme sola con las trocas dando vueltas por el pueblo. Sobre todo, por la amenaza. Pensó en llamar a su jefe de allá, de la maquila, y pedir el día, pero al final se fue. «Estaré bien, mami, no te preocupes», le dije en la parada del camión, con el amanecer pálido sobre nosotras. Nos despedimos con un beso, como cualquier otro día. Ni idea de que no volveríamos a vernos. Al menos no en persona, porque al siguiente domingo no regresó. Le pidieron trabajar horas extra el fin de semana. Volvió cuando todo había pasado.

Almorcé dos tazas de café. Las necesitaba. Las camionetas fueron y vinieron por la terracería, alrededor de la casa, toda la noche. Lo hacían a propósito, para robarnos el sueño. Para fastidiarnos y que les vendiéramos la tierra de ito Juan. Pero no lo haríamos. Cuando se fueron, me puse tu sudadera del Cruz Azul y a darle. Desde que te fuiste la usé. Me recordaba que estabas en el norte, viendo por nosotras. Al principio olía a ti, pero con las lavadas pronto olió a ropa nomás. Y ese día te necesitaba más que otros y quería sentirte cerca.

Escombraba el cuarto de los abuelitos y entonces lo hallé. Llevaba semanas dejándolo para luego, porque no podía entrar a la habitación sin llorar. No quería aceptar su ausencia. Pero ya ibas a llegar, para ayudarnos con lo del terreno, ¿y dónde iban a dormir tú y Norma, y Juanito? Levanté todo y barrí y trapeé sin parar de llorar. Cada barrida, cada trapeada, quemaba con cloro mi corazón, me lavaba la pena. Levanté sus cosas una por una, acariciándolas. Y así lo encontré, refundido en una caja llena de fotos viejas: el collar de ita Tonantzin, una figurita de barro añejo con forma de árbol de la vida. Te has de acordar: siempre lo trae puesto en las fotos. Lo sostuve con la palma abierta para verlo bien. Y como que se sentía vivo, como si tuviera en la mano una lagartija. Le tomé una foto y le escribí a mamá: «Mira lo que apareció». Esperaba un audio, una anécdota por respuesta, pero ya ves.... No la dejaban usar el celular si estaba trabajando. Me contestó al otro día: «El collar de mamá Tona.... Es un amuleto, hija, quédatelo. Te va a proteger». Y eso hice. Lo demás lo doné a la parroquia.

Volví a la iglesia saliendo de la escuela. La parroquia había conseguido que una maestra de teatro viniera de la ciudad por las tardes, para ayudar al grupo juvenil a montar el Viacrucis. Yo me había apuntado, así que atravesé el atrio a la sombra de los ocotes, hasta llegar al salón de usos múltiples del traspatio. Los vi hacer el calentamiento y me apuré.

La maestra nos puso un reto nuevo: improvisar una escena con algo que lleváramos en la bolsa del pantalón. Sin diálogos ni compañeros, sólo yo y lo que llevara. Y lo único que tenía era el collar. Cuando fue mi turno pasé al frente. La maestra aplaudió: corría ya mi tiempo. Tomé el árbol de la vida entre mis manos, como si fuera un pájaro herido. Aplaudió de nuevo, y con ella mis compañeros. El pájaro se convirtió en un bebé —imaginé que era tu hijo Juanito, mi sobrino—y yo lo llevé a mi pecho y lo arrullé con una canción. Otra ronda de aplausos. Me vi arrullando las cenizas de ito Juan. Sentí cómo me brotaban las lágrimas. Aplaudieron una última vez. Las cenizas fueron entonces una semilla de ceiba. Me hinqué, hice como si la plantara en el piso. La regué con mis lágrimas. Luego me levanté con los ojos cerrados, extendiendo los brazos hacia el cielo. Imaginé que un árbol brotaba de la semilla, como si fuera un chorro de agua escupido por una fuente.

Y así pasó, fuera de mi imaginación. La semilla estalló y se hizo una ceiba que llenó todo el salón. La maestra y el grupo lo vieron también. Y todo se detuvo. Silencio, miradas de asombro. Algunos se pusieron de rodillas y empezaron a rezar. No tardó nada en correrse la voz.

Toda la noche le di vueltas a lo de la ceiba. Quería una explicación.

Hasta pasé a la iglesia al otro día, antes de clases, para ver si había sido real eso de que apareciera nomás con imaginarlo. ¿Y qué crees? La ceiba todavía estaba ahí, quebrando la loza con sus raíces, rozando el techo con sus ramas. La rodeaba un grupo de rezanderas que, entre murmullos, pasaban las cuentas de sus rosarios. No era un retoño, sino un árbol maduro, con su corteza de piel de lagartija toda llena de espinas y sus ramas colgando hacia abajo, cual manos extendidas hacia las mujeres que le rezaban. Y colgado de una de ellas, como si la ceiba lo alzara del piso, estaba el collar de ita Tonantzin. De la impresión lo había dejado el día anterior. No sé cómo nadie lo halló. Lo agarré y lo tuve de nuevo.

«Cipactli, ¿qué piensas de eso?».

Era el profe de sociales, el mismo que igual te dio clases. Ya sabes quién: playeras del Che todos los días, y gorrita zapatista que nunca se quita. Volví de mi lelera.

«¿Que qué, profe?».

«¿Qué piensas de la expropiación ejidal de 1990? San Miguel Ototipac perdió la mitad de sus tierras comunales para que se construyera el periférico. De eso ha sido toda la clase…».

Al profe siempre le gustó hablar de política en palabras enredadas. Y si me preguntaba a mí era porque yo sabía el tipo de respuestas que le gustaban y cómo decirlas. Me conoces: siempre fui buena para hablar, desde chiquita. Siempre me pusieron a declamar el juramento a la bandera, a recitar poemas el día de las madres y esas cosas. Pero esa mañana no hallé palabras. La lengua se me hizo un nudo y sólo atiné a ver por la ventana, más allá de las canchas y las milpas, hacia el terreno de ito Juan.

El profe esperó.

Escupí una respuesta:

«Que es una mamada».

Igual y de coraje me llevé la mano al collar de ita Tonantzin. Entonces supe qué hacer.

Me fui derechito al acahual de don Ramiro cuando acabaron las clases. Estaba seco seco de tanto químico. Era el lugar perfecto para probar. Puse el collar sobre la tierra, cerré los ojos, e imaginé un jardín crecer sobre el terreno. Cuando los abrí fue como ver uno de esos documentales que ponía la maestra de biología, ¿te acuerdas? Era una de esas escenas donde ves pasar meses en unos cuantos segundos. De la tierra, reseca como piel de culebra, nacieron brotes de plantitas y crecieron en retoños y acabaron hechos una arboleda. Cuando alcé el collar, el jardín no se desvaneció, como tampoco hizo la ceiba allá en la iglesia.

Don Ramiro estuvo muy contento el resto de la semana. Fue a la iglesia, a darle gracias a la Virgencita por el milagro y hasta se echó para atrás con la venta de su parcela que la inmobiliaria insistía en adquirir. Le mandaron a los hombres de las trocas, a disque negociar, pero entonces ya se hablaba de la ceiba—ya sabes: chisme de pueblo—y con lo del terreno, el asunto escaló a milagro. Todo el pueblo estaba metido en la iglesia. Empezó a llegar gente de otros lados. Hasta vino el padre desde la ciudad, a media semana, aunque no le tocara oficiar misa, nomás a ver si era verdad eso que le decían por teléfono. Era tanta la gente que nadie tuvo miedo a los hombres de la inmobiliaria, ni aunque llegaron armados. Que se iba a hacer una capilla, que debía venir el obispo declarar santo el lugar. No se hablaba de otra cosa.

Pero yo pensaba en algo más: el terreno de ito Juan. Ya estaba bardeado y tenía un letrero que decía «Próximamente: Jardines de Gaia. Tu paraíso ecológico». Ya lo habían allanado para empezar a construir. Fui esa misma noche. Logré colarme por las calles sin toparme con las trocas, y escalar el paredón.

Habrías llorado al mirarlo. ¿Te acuerdas del cazahuite que crecía grande en la esquina, donde anidaban las golondrinas? ¿Y del níspero que trepábamos cuando éramos niños? Ya no estaban. Ya no había nada. El tecorral donde vivían las lagartijas, la lomita que se llenaba de hongos con las lluvias, el jacal donde se escondían los cacomixtles... Nada. Una extensión siniestra, de arena aplanada a la perfección, era todo lo que iluminaba la luz pálida de los reflectores.

Y el muro de concreto alrededor. La parcela de nuestro abuelito destazada en lotes, lista para la obra.

Eché un vistazo a la caseta del velador: la ventana destellaba en azul. Tenía la tele prendida. Caminé hasta el centro del terreno, puse el collar sobre la tierra y dejé volar mi imaginación.

Del suelo emergieron los brotes, las hojitas.

Ni tú ni yo conocimos a ita Tonantzin más que en fotos viejas. Pero a mí me gustaba preguntarle por ella a ito Juan. Que cómo era, que cómo hablaba, que qué hacía.

«Era una mujer muy sabia, mijita, muy buena para las plantas», me contestaba y luego se arrancaba a contarme de su vida. Así supe quién era ella, lo que hacía. Ayudó a nacer a prácticamente todos en el pueblo. Curaba a los necesitados, nomás por buena gente, sin cobrar jamás un solo peso. Y todo con hierbas, piedras y ensalmos, como las curanderas de las leyendas.

Nuestro abuelito la extrañaba mucho. Se lo sentía en la voz cada que me hablaba de ella. Pero nunca se ponía triste, al revés: le brotaba la alegría. Un día le pregunté el motivo. «Es que sigue aquí conmigo, con ustedes, hija. Nunca nos deja». Eso fue lo que me dijo. Estábamos en su terreno, juntando hongos, y pensé que hablaba en sentido figurado, como quien dice que un ser amado vive en su corazón luego de fallecer. Pero no.

La inmobiliaria metió otra vez la maquinaria para limpiar el pedazo de monte que había crecido de la noche a la mañana. Mientras tanto, la gente se apiñonaba afuera del terreno, frente al portón; era el tercer «milagro» en poco más de una semana. El velador juró haberlo visto con sus propios ojos: vegetación creciendo de la nada, árboles alzándose en segundos a alturas de décadas, hierbas del tiempo de las abuelas, que ya casi no se veían, brotando por montones, flores reventando de la nada cual cohetones de fiesta hechos de pétalos. Lo contó todo y renunció para irse de peregrinación a Juquila.

Sepa cómo no me vio a mí también, ahí parada, con mi sonrisota en medio de aquella fiesta de plantas. Lo contó todo, pero sólo los del grupo de teatro sabían quién hacía la magia, el milagro o lo que fuera. Claro que lo soltaron, hablaron de la muchachita y del amuleto del árbol de la vida. Pero nadie les hizo caso. Supongo que la gente prefería creer en los poderes de la Virgen y, por mí, mejor.

Al principio importó poco lo que hice. La inmobiliaria aplanó otra vez el terreno en un solo día. Les urgía empezar a construir, porque eso significaría que ya eran dueños de nuestra tierra, que no importaba el litigio. Pero yo estaba dispuesta a usar el collar una y otra vez, las que fueran necesarias. Usaría su magia, porque el terreno era de nuestros abuelitos y querían robarlo. Como habían hecho antes con tantas otras familias del pueblo y hasta con los ejidos comunales de la falda del cerro. Entonces—en realidad, hace no mucho—se aprovecharon de nuestra falta de dinero y de nuestros pleitos, de la tranza del gobierno para hacer el cambio de uso de suelo. Después, llenaron el pueblo de trocas con hombres armados y, así, también se aprovecharon de nuestro miedo. Y ahora ito Juan había muerto y querían quedarse con su terreno. Querían arrebatarnos su tierra, su recuerdo, mas yo no los dejaría.

Volví esa misma noche. Ya acampaba el gentío afuera del portón, guadalupanos con esperanzas de atestiguar el milagro. Los rodeé y seguí el muro, en busca de un lugar oscuro donde poder trepar sin ser vista. Y lo encontré, casi en la esquina. ¿Te acuerdas del ahuehuete del terreno de junto? Ahí mero. Su sombra oscurecía por completo la pared. Fue como si me leyeran la mente lo de teatro: ya estaban ahí, esperándome. Con su ayuda, subir fue mucho más fácil y pronto estuvimos dentro. El nuevo velador debió estar en el baño o algo así, pues no estaba por ninguna parte. Volví a poner el collar en el centro del terreno y otra vez imaginé, esta vez algo más vasto.

Un bosque se alzó del suelo.

A la mañana siguiente llegué tarde a la prepa. Una de las camionetas de la inmobiliaria esperó afuera de la casa hasta bien entrada la mañana. Pensé que no se atreverían a entrar, no con el pueblo tan alborotado, tan despierto por lo de los milagros. De todas formas esperé aún después que se fueran. Cuando por fin salí, vi el rayón sobre el portón: «te vamos a chingar si no le paras». Traté de calmarme. «No van a hacer nada, Cipactli, no van a hacer nada», me decía. Pero me temblaba todo el cuerpo y, cuando me encaminé a la escuela, cualquier ruidito me hacía saltar a esconderme.

Volví esa noche. Y también la siguiente y la siguiente. Las amenazas no pararon. Yo tampoco. No podía dejarles el terreno de nuestros abuelitos. Y ya sabían que era yo, así que dormí en la parroquia para estar segura. Estaba abierta todo el día y toda la noche, porque peregrinos de otros pueblos y hasta de la ciudad venían a ver los milagros. La inmobiliaria trajo más y más hombres armados para mantenerlos fuera del terreno. Se hizo más difícil entrar, pero el grupo de teatro me esperó cada noche y siempre pudimos colarnos entre el gentío y saltar la barda sin ser vistos. Cada mañana aparecía un bosque cubría el terreno. Y para cuando anochecía, lo habían talado de nuevo.

Empecé a quedarme dormida en clase, por las desveladas. No estaba al cien, pero pensaba que ya mero se rendiría la inmobiliaria, pues ya el obispo presionaba allá en la ciudad a la gente de la inmobiliaria y acá en el pueblo, ya se hablaba de hacerle un santuario a la Virgen ahí, en el terreno del abuelo, que daban por santo de tanta maravilla ocurrida los últimos días. Pero también porque, ¿cuánto habría gastado ya la inmobiliaria? No podrían rentar todos esos trascabos y aplanadoras para siempre. Tenían que echarse para atrás, algún día. Eso pensaba aquella última noche, mientras subía la barda con ayuda de un par de compañeros del grupo de teatro.

Salté al otro lado y eché un ojo a la cabina del velador. No había nadie. Afuera del muro, sólo silencio, ni oraciones ni canciones de iglesia, como las noches anteriores. Y no me pareció raro, no sé por qué. Caminé hasta el centro del terreno bajo la luz fantasmagórica de los reflectores. Puse el collar sobre la tierra y entonces oí el griterío: eran mis compañeros, eran advertencias. Demasiado tarde: algo me atravesó por la espalda.

No supe dónde estaba. No sentí frío ni calor. Todo era oscuro y no sentía mi cuerpo. Algo me apretaba por todas partes y no podía moverme o, mejor dicho, no tenía cuerpo que mover. Estuve así no sé cuánto, tratando de entender. Entonces llegaron los susurros, como siseos de serpiente: «Cipactli... Ci-pac-tli». Y de alguna forma reconocí esas voces: eran las raíces del níspero, del cazahuite, de los ocotes destazados por los trascabos, la parte subterránea de los hongos que ya no crecerían, las tuzas, las lombrices, las lagartijas, todos los animalitos sepultados en sus madrigueras por las aplanadoras. «Ci-pac-tli», susurraban en una madeja de voces. Después de un rato reconocí entre ellas las voces humanas: nuestras ancestras. Mujeres viejas, antiguas, me llamaban: «Cipactli... Ci-pac-tli».

Mis compañeros alcanzaron a escapar, pero a mí me tiraron aquí mismo, en una zanja. El collar se rompió en mi puño, mas ya no lo necesitaba. Las voces y yo alzamos el bosque noche tras noche. Cada mañana, ahí estaba: enorme, frondoso. No se lo pudieron explicar jamás los de la inmobiliaria. Como tampoco pudieron explicar qué hacían ahí mis restos, en la parcela.

El grupo de teatro contó la versión conveniente, la que se ha hecho verdad de tanta repetición: nos escapamos de noche para ver el milagro con nuestros propios ojos. Nos colamos sin ser vistos. Adentro estaban los hombres armados, y nos obligaron a detenernos. No lo hicimos. A ellos los detuvieron, a mí.... Me hicieron otras cosas. Quise defenderme y me golpearon. Mis amigos lucharon para zafarse y detenerlos. Luego, disparos. Ellos escaparon; yo no. Y nadie volvió a verme jamás. Los de la inmobiliaria no pudieron probar su inocencia. ¿Qué iban a decir? ¿Que tenían paramilitares en el pueblo? ¿Que una bruja les crecía árboles en el terreno cada noche para que no construyeran?

La gente se puso furiosa. Tantos abusos, tanto miedo.... Fui la gota que derramó el vaso. Tomaron el terreno del abuelo y pintaron consignas de protesta en el paredón. Hicieron un plantón frente al palacio municipal. Cerraron autopistas. Hicieron una marcha hasta la capital y tomaron las oficinas de la inmobiliaria. La cosa se fue a los noticieros nacionales. A las autoridades no les quedó de otra más que investigar. Y así dieron con mis restos. Pero eso tú ya lo viste, hermano, ya habías regresado del norte. Ya te tocó ver cómo se fue, por fin, la inmobiliaria.

Sólo me arrepiento de haberme ido así, sin decirle adiós a mamá. Le rompió el corazón identificar mis restos. Cómo quisiera decirle que no me fui, que estoy aquí. Quisiera que pudieras oírme, hermano, cada que vienes al terreno del abuelo. Pero lo sé: sientes el cariño que te hago llegar en el aroma de las flores, en el húmedo de la tierra y en la sombra refrescante de los árboles. Todo eso lo hago para ustedes. Y me gusta cuando juegas con Juanito, mi sobrino, sobre mí. Adoro escucharles la risa, a ti y a mamá. Aun así, cómo quisiera que pudieras escuchar todo esto, como cuando éramos niños y te contaba cuentos para dormirte. Quisiera tener mi voz, hablar con palabras de viento y susurrarte al oído: «Oye, no me fui, no me mataron, hermanito, no de verdad». Decirte que vivo en cada palmo de esta tierra trabajada con tanto amor por el abuelo. Decirte que, como ita Tonantzin y las mujeres antes de ella, me hice una con el suelo.

Guillermo G. Mendoza is a Mexican writer from Orizaba, México. He's also both a teacher and a literary researcher. When not involved with literature, he can be found hiking and cycling. His story "The Heart of the Land" got published in Android Press' *Bioluminescent: A Lunarpunk Anthology* in 2023. You can find him on Twitter at @Momentanium.

The Spanish version of "Una con el suelo" was edited by Laura Martínez-Lara.

That Time My Grandfather Got Lost in the Translations of the Word 'Death'

Oluwatomiwa Ajeigbe

Have you ever seen a behemoth? The ones brought in by the foreigners
after the silent war? I was a boy, eight, nine years old, when I saw it.
Have you ever seen a forest catch fire? Your entire village's herd destroyed
in an instant? Of course not. The behemoth was eight feet tall & breathed fire.
It's body was made of metal and painted black. The behemoth destroyed our land,
making it impossible to sow. There was no harvest that year. Do you know what we did?
We built a behemoth of our own. An ugly thing, powered by sunlight and unlike the original,
our behemoth required piloting. I was chosen to ride the thing. It was a terribly tight fit.
But I managed. The behemoth struck me but our machine held its own. When it spat fire,
I shot water from my chest. When it tried to uproot trees, I bound it with strong cords.
I pushed it away, away from the village, deep into the hills. Then I hit it until it fell apart.
That was when I thought I would die. Nobody to help. My own behemoth was heating up.
Do you know what I did? I prayed. Or tried to. But I couldn't remember the word for death.
I was praying to our ancestors for a swift death but the word was replaced
by the foreigners tongue. Ha. Obviously, I survived. But I sat there in pain and fear,
because they just didn't try to destroy and steal our land but they tried to take our language.
Do you know what the word for death is? You don't? Lean closer and I'll tell you . . . .

Oluwatomiwa Ajeigbe is writer of the dark and fantastical, a poet, and a reluctant mathematician. He has poetry and fiction published or forthcoming in *F&SF*, *Podcastle*, *Beneath Ceaseless Skies*, *Lightspeed*, *Anathema Spec*, *FANTASY* and elsewhere. When he's not writing about malfunctioning robots or crazed gods, he can be found doing whatever people do on Twitter at @OluwaSigma. He writes from a room with broken windowpanes in Lagos, Nigeria.

It's In the Blood

Susan Kaye Quinn

The days were more dear now.

She could give minutes to the snapdragons, pruning their spent blooms and freeing the stems to flower again. Or spend an hour with her glasses and notebook, hoping for a tufted titmouse to report to the lost species trackers.

Or she could stay inside on Shredder and save a person's life.

She plucked a call from the ether. Shredder's voice channel gave them privacy, no storage or data mining for the AI, and it dumped as soon as the call was over. But there were hundreds of callers and who she connected to was random, a cosmic lottery no more fair than the Fates spinning the wheel, but there wasn't a better way. Not yet.

"Smilin' Charlie's Energy Pills," she intoned. "We've got what you need to recharge your life! How are you doing to today?"

"I'm . . . okay." English, so no AI-translator echo on top of their words. The voice was young, but then they all were compared to her.

"I bet you need some recharging! I can set you up with our free starter kit of a month's worth of energy at no price today. How does that sound?" She wished they were real. She'd sign up herself.

"I . . . I was told to ask for Grandma Maisy."

"Well, we don't have any Grandma Maisy here, but I can assure you, I'm fully qualified to take care of you." The schtick was rough some days, but it was important to delay, so Salomé could validate the call, no voice manipulation or tracing, make sure it was someone desperate for help, not the police. Or worse, the Department of Biological Integrity.

"I was told I should ask twice. For Grandma Maisy." Hope was leaking out of their young voice like the last breath leaving a body.

"Maisy is a funny name." Which always brought her a smile, given she'd picked it. "Kinda old-fashioned. How old do you think that name is?"

"Before plastic." A common-enough saying, but strange enough in context to work as old-school security. Plus, the all-clear had come in from Salomé.

Her shoulders relaxed. "That's right." She used her normal voice, the one that didn't sound like she was selling magic pills, when in fact, she was now free to share the *real* magic. The kind that worked. "Before plastic.

You're not looking for more energy—you're looking for a *cure.* Isn't that right?"

"Are you Grandma Maisy?"

"I am." Close enough.

"I've got three kids, Maisy. All depending on me. Not all mine, either, but they've already lost too much."

"They can't afford to lose you too." She said it strong. People didn't need to justify it to her, but they always tried. Which was one way to tell they were real. The Bio Integrity thugs always assumed everyone was as slimy and manipulative as they were. She'd been able to spot them 10/10 so far.

"Does it actually work?"

The only real question. "It does. But there are some risks." She listed them off. Full disclosure. More than you'd get in a clinical trial, which this was, only the illegal kind. A global operation that circumvented the official channels, given they'd been taken over by the sort of people whose politics were responsible for the carnage she was trying to stop. If they got hold of her magic—and it didn't belong to her, nor did she invent it, but she was holding together the operation to quietly proliferate the hell out of it—the powerful would shut it all down before she could blink. They were all-in on necropolitics, using their power to decide who deserved to die so the rest, including them, could continue to live in the style to which they'd become accustomed. The necropoliticians would take her magic pills, test them on a few unfortunates, then hoard it for themselves, their cronies, sell it to the well-connected and the wealthy. As if they couldn't buy plastic-free livers any day of the week. Everybody lived in the ubiquitous soup of microplastics, but some people had a bigger lifeboat than others.

She was selling tickets to the biggest lifeboat of all. Or rather, giving them away.

But only to a few, for now: the ones the Fates had selected. She was good at keeping the cops out, but she couldn't bear to decide which of the normies would live. Too heavy of a burden, on top of everything else. She was glad for the randomness and secrecy of Shredder.

She processed the caller through and handed off the order to Salomé. She was in Colombia, but they had labs on every continent now, and in most countries with populations over 50M. Local shipping was key—avoiding customs meant higher likelihood of the capsules reaching the caller before they expired. It was a miracle the cure worked at all, but a strong secondary miracle had made the bio-active materials transportable in little room-temperature capsules you could slide into a box and send anywhere that shipping reached.

She fielded three more callers before Salomé broke in, the translator's English heavy over her whispered Spanish. "Sorry to interrupt, but Diego wants to talk."

"Is there a problem?" Diego was her master biologist, the inventor of the magic cure for plastic liver. He also tracked all the results of their illegal clinical trial.

"He wouldn't say."

"Put him through." She waited while the line clicked over.

"Maisy, hello, how are ya this fine day?" Diego wasn't his name any more than hers was Maisy, but she knew people who knew people who vouched for his bonafides. That's how it all started.

"As well as can be expected. Tell me there's nothing wrong, and I'll feel better."

"I have too many capsules."

"That doesn't sound like a problem." She squeezed her eyes shut and rubbed her forehead because she knew better.

"They're sitting in the labs. *Spoiling,* Maisy. You know this."

"I'm training Salomé. She'll be ready soon. I've got trainee candidates lined up in Brazil and Nigeria, next. And we've got . . . ." Fatigue clouded her brain for a moment. "Almost a hundred volunteers on intake now? We're fielding thousands of calls a day, Diego."

"It's not enough. You know this, too."

"I know this," she admitted. The weight of it suffocated her, all day and night. Worse when she thought about it.

"We need to go public," Diego said.

Not this again. "We're not ready."

"We are."

"Bio Integrity will shut us down."

"Only in America—"

"Which happens to be where I live. Besides, the Ministério da Biologia will do the same in Brazil. The Australian Institute for Population Monitoring will have a field day. I can't even think about the Russians. *Diego . . . .*" They'd had this fight so many times, and her energy wasn't there for it. The fatigue got worse every day. She couldn't even keep her breakfast down lately, so she skipped it this morning, but that left her empty and weak. "We're not ready."

"Maisy, my dear friend...." They had never met, but that didn't matter. "*You* are not ready. But we are."

"That's not fair."

"But it *is* true."

She balled up her fist, wanting to smash the button to disconnect the call. But even that took too much. Her shoulders slumped. "I'll think about it." He didn't need her permission for anything...but he was asking for her blessing. And that chewed her up inside.

"Are you okay?"

"Worse now, thanks for asking."

"Maisy—"

"I need to go." She clicked off the call and crumpled head-down on the table. One breath, two. She lay there until she knew that if she didn't move, everything in her would stiffen. Slowly, she rose. The bed beckoned, and a nap might do her good, but the garden would do her better. She struggled to pull her socks over her ankles, which were swollen to unrecognizable lumps, but at least her loose shoes still fit. Her garden gloves and hat hung by the door, and she'd need those to keep the blazing sun from cooking her too fast. She checked the air quality before she ventured out, not that a slow death by air pollution would matter at this stage. But an asthma attack wouldn't do her any favors.

She brought a small basket, in case there was any harvesting to be done. Then she shuffled down the sidewalk to the community garden. It wasn't far, but she had to stop twice to catch her breath. It was a brutal metric. An unforgiving one, impossible to ignore. But she tried.

A few neighbors were at the garden, which was already bursting with the fruits of summer. A micro-utopia. She snagged a kneeler from the front and found a spot alone in the forest of tomato plants. It was well past noon, so one row shaded the next, and down between them, she could dig her hands into the dirt, finding a slow peace in uprooting the weeds that didn't belong and gently plucking the cherry reds from the vines. If they weren't quite ripe, they wouldn't release, but the ones whose time had come, who had reached their peak, let go so easy they almost fell off the vine with the slightest nudge.

Maybe Diego was right. Maybe it was time to let go.

This project was the last of many acts she'd taken to heal the Earth and its beings of all the harms done. If they'd stopped plastic production entirely a decade ago, that still wouldn't have been enough, and they hadn't even done that. Instead, the necropoliticians decided that bodies stuffed with microplastics just meant a shorter lifetime for some. Sorry about your luck. The rich were fine, of course, able to swap out for lab-grown livers once theirs became hopelessly scarred. Five years or fifty million breaths: time for a filter change!

The rich got them like clockwork. Some folks in the middle were able to "work for their liver." But the rest of the world? Couldn't afford a trip to the doctor much less a lab-grown miracle.

Then Diego and his pills showed up in her circles, and she had another chance to save the world, one life at a time. She didn't understand all the tech—some combo of plastic-eating single-celled creatures and genetic-mod technology that Diego called an *evolvant*—but in the end, it was simple. A part of you wasn't *you* anymore, but collection of organisms adapted to thrive in the Anthropocene, feasting on the toxins that would kill you otherwise. A biological cyborg. *Mutant.* But the result was clear: you got your life back. The world had become a chemical soup that eventually drowned everyone, one way or another, but you would be adapted to survive.

Not that it was an easy process, transforming an internal organ, one cell at a time. Sometimes it didn't work. They screened for age and counter-indicated conditions. Because this was only a cure for those who weren't too far gone already.

Like her.

Too bad that train had left the station before she could get onboard.

Still, it gave her something useful to do. Like picking cherry tomatoes or tracking the birds. Only this was more powerful. Probably the best thing she'd ever done.

"Devika! Are you okay?" Her friend Ezra rushed through the tomato forest, concern crinkling up that young dark-skinned face.

"I'm fine. I'm fine." She waved him off.

"You don't look fine." He got more concerned as he knelt down beside her.

She was quite a sight, a heap of bones and tired, swollen flesh, a smattering of tomatoes in her basket and weed carnage at her feet. "Just sitting in the dirt with the tomatoes. Nothing to see here."

He scowled. "Let me help you up."

She wasn't ready to leave, but Ezra would fuss, and she didn't have energy for that, either. She gave him her hand, but he bent down with those youthful muscles and practically scooped her out of the soil. She laughed a little as he set her on her feet, but then the dizziness made her wobble.

"That's it," he said. "I'm taking you home."

"Alright." No sense in fighting it. And with his arm firm at her back, she was steady. Wouldn't even have to stop to catch her breath.

"You've got the liver, don't you?" Ezra said quietly on the way.

"Well, everyone does." She wheezed a little. "Why should I be any different?"

"You should try those pills." He watched the sidewalk for cracks that might be hazardous to her.

His words drew her gaze. "What pills?"

"You haven't heard? It's a cure. A *real* one."

"Sounds like snake oil to me." But her heart was thrumming.

He dipped his head and lowered his voice. "They fixed my cousin. Complete reversal. You can't get the pills from any doctor, but they're the real deal. I can get them for you."

"Can you, now?"

His fervent nod settled something deep in her bones. Ezra was quiet until they got to her door. "You want me to come in?"

"Ezra, I'm fine."

"I'll get you those pills." He was very serious now. "You just say the word. And don't be stubborn, Ms. Patel. I've got more stubborn than you. I'll wear you down."

She smiled. "Now, that's a threat." But she waved him off again. She needed some time alone before she broke the news to him—that even the miracle cure was too late for her. "Give me a minute to rest, then you come back. We'll have ourselves a chat."

He nodded his acceptance.

She'd left all her energy at the garden, and without Ezra's help, it was rough getting to her desk, but she made it.

She'd wanted to wait until they'd built up enough of a network that she could be sure no one could shut it down. Or even better, wait until the necropoliticians were shoved out of power again, at least in her country, because then they could really do something, with the right folks in charge. In the meantime, she'd spent all her effort on getting the pills to whoever they could. But if word of them had spread so far that they were showing up in her own backyard . . . maybe the network had grown big enough. Maybe people like her friend Ezra would see it through.

She mustered her energy and got on Shredder. Direct to Diego.

"Maisy! It's good to hear from you." He was surprised.

"Diego, I've been trying to stop the bleeding, all this time."

"*What?*" His alarm blasted through.

"I'm speaking metaphorically."

"Oh."

"When you're in an emergency, it's important to stop the bleeding, but at some point, that doesn't matter. At some point, you have to stop patching up the wounds and take away the butcher knife."

"I'm not sure I follow." He sounded worried for her mental health. But that was the only kind she had.

"It's time to go public."

"Really? You mean it?"

She really did. "You invented this thing. You built a worldwide network to get it to the people who need it most. You waited and played it smart and now . . . ." The dizziness was making her head spin. "Tell the world, Diego. Tell them what you've done." She propped her head on her hands to keep it from swimming. "What's your name, sweetie?" Her voice was slurring. She could hear it. "Your real one."

"Patrick."

"Nice to meet you, Patrick." It came out a wheeze. "My name's Devika." And then she felt something slipping away. She tried to close the call, but she missed the button on the way down into blackness.

She awoke to the taste of metal and Ezra's smiling face.

"Hey." Her throat felt thick, and she coughed.

He helped her with water. "The docs said you might be waking up soon. Glad I was here to see it."

She patted his hand to show she could hold the glass of water and straw herself. "You brought me to the hospital?" She couldn't remember a damn thing. But Ezra must have come back for her and brought her in. Not that it would help.

He nodded. A bit of smile snuck onto his face. "I bet you don't remember much."

"Ezra, I don't remember anything." She was in a hospital bed. The yellow walls of her room were dotted with monitors and their silent blips.

"You could have told me, you know." His smile got stronger. "That you were Grandma Maisy."

"Oh. That." She took another long drink of water. Then she frowned. "Wait, how did you. . . ." Her brain felt like it had been packed with cotton.

"A lot's happened in the last ten days."

"Ten *what*." She leaned over to set down her glass, and a sharp pinch stabbed her stomach. She winced and cradled her hand to it. "What the—"

"Take it easy." Ezra was on his feet now, like he might barricade her from getting out of bed. "The doc said it would hurt some as the anesthetic wore off."

She stared at him, like he was speaking German with the translator off. Then she gingerly poked around her stomach and a staccato of dulled pain raced across her middle. She dug around the tangle of blankets and sheets and hospital gown, not caring if she was flashing poor Ezra with her wrinkly old body, but when she got to skin, she could hardly take it in.

The upside-down "T" of a liver transplant incision splayed across her abdomen, stapled together like a railroad track of flesh. She didn't believe it until she passed her hand gently over it, the touch bringing the winces of pain a little sharper.

She dropped her gown and looked up. "How?" It was the only

word her brain could form.

"Turns out there's a lot of folks who want Grandma Maisy to have a new liver." He looked fit to burst with that smile. "'Course, I was the one who told them to keep you out, otherwise you might have some sass about it."

She just sat there with her mouth hanging open.

He cocked his head. "I know what you really want to know."

"You do?" She still had not a single thought in her head but wonder.

Ezra settled back in his chair and scratched his chin. "Devika would want to know the tomato harvest is coming quite nicely."

Some of her senses were coming back to her. "And Grandma Maisy?"

He smirked. "She'd like to know her magic pills are in short supply, but every country on Earth has been forced to fund production to meet the need. The network Grandma Maisy built—it's too big, too pervasive, too connected everywhere. The first day of protests... you'll have to go back and watch. But the politicians had no choice."

"Oh." She eased back to rest on her pillow, ginger with her newly stapled stomach. "You're saying it worked."

"I'm saying it worked. And Patrick says hello." His smile was getting downright infectious.

"Well, all right, then." She blinked several more times before it truly sunk in. "Maybe now I'll have time to tend my flowers." Or count the birds. Or watch this miracle unfold and know that she'd done something good. Something real.

"I'd say you've earned your retirement."

She didn't know if she was ready for *that*.

But she was surprised to find the days were even more precious when you suddenly had a lot more of them.

Susan Kaye Quinn is an environmental engineer/rocket scientist turned speculative fiction author who now uses her PhD to invent cool stuff in books. Her works range from hopepunk climate fiction to gritty cyberpunk to steampunk romance. Her short fiction can be found in *DreamForge*, *Grist*, *Little Blue Planet*, and more. All her novels and short fiction can be found on her website: www.susankayequinn.com.

Fixing the System in Tilt Town

Kat Murray

When I was little, my parents died trying to reach Lady Luck. My brother Maynard says the journey was hard back then. These days, it's easier for people to worship at her feet.

What she demands as sacrifice isn't so straightforward.

"There's *nothing* for him in this town." Maynard's voice is bitter as he watches Clay skip off to school on his ninth birthday. My nephew is a sweet boy, all shining hazel eyes under a thatch of curly dark hair that reminds us of his late mother. She died when Lady Luck frowned on her, but nobody mentions that. It's just one of those things.

A few days ago, I tried to show Clay how I wanted to streamline the house's microfiltration system, but Maynard told me to cut that shit out. Clay is destined for greater things. In two months, the boy will enter the education lottery and then he might be able to get out of here.

"It's not fair," Maynard continues. "Getting that bitch Luck to smile ain't easy for people like me. Not these days."

My brother lapses into a stony silence. I'm loath to break it. I turn my eyes without moving my head, checking on Gran. She's blessedly asleep.

Maynard picks up one of my stray models I meant to put away. Wires twist intricately through a pair of oversized buttons, each one representing airflow—the beginnings of an idea I have, if I ever get to design it. Maynard's broad thumb crushes the delicate thing. Wires bend beyond recognition as he continues to ruminate.

"Clay needs an extra boost," he declares. "Something to get him through that lottery and into the City, where he'll have more chances."

Under the table where my brother can't see, I let my hands and toes fidget. "A visit to Lady Luck?" I whisper.

"Damn straight." Maynard bares yellowed teeth in a kind of smile. "We'll leave in three days."

We?

Maynard reveals more of his teeth as he preempts my next question. "You're coming with me, Cassie. Gran, too."

"What about Clay?" I ask.

"He'll stay in town. It isn't a problem finding someone to look after *him* for a month."

Once my brother makes a decision, nothing sways him. Fear of the unknown rivets me to the hard plastic chair. But a shiver of excitement lurks underneath.

I've always wanted to leave town. There's nothing for me here, either.

The hours tick down to our departure. I can't shake my unease. I've mapped out our journey a dozen times, tracing the way past other towns all the way to the ocean. Lady Luck lives at the edge of the water, near enough the City to constantly watch over its unmoving houses, high walls, and thick gates.

To get to her, we'll have to pass perilously near Tilt Town.

Tilter streets are crooked gashes across steep hills, nothing like the neat layout of normal towns. Instead of balancing on treads and wheels, their dwellings cling to the soil any which way they can, because the earth often shifts underneath Tilt Town.

That's how the place got its name. The inhabitants must constantly be ready to readjust the slant of their living quarters, to recut stilts and shore up bedrooms and kitchens so they can sleep and eat without rolling sideways.

Maynard says the Tilters don't worship Lady Luck hard enough, even though they practically live at her feet, and that's why none of them are successful. When I misbehaved as a kid—which was often—he'd threaten to send me there. Now, even though I'm long past the days of overt meltdowns, the thought of Tilt Town makes me shiver.

Across the room, near the driver's capsule, Gran moans from her recliner. I'm glad for an excuse to fold the map. The house sways slightly on its treads as I fetch a precious measure of water. Maynard says it doesn't matter at this point if Gran ingests microplastics, so he forbade me to use the house's inbuilt filtering system for her. Instead, I take out one of my homemade contraptions, decanting a small amount into Gran's favorite cup. Her lips press against worn enamel. She can barely manage to drink by herself these days.

I wish Gran and I could stay behind with Clay, but Maynard is right. Nobody here would take us in.

I hold Gran's bony hand and explain our upcoming journey. With her, I always presume competence. I taught Clay to do the same, even though Gran is mostly listless, gazing out the window into our yard, where we manage to cultivate a crop of hardy vegetables.

But when I tell Gran we're going to see Lady Luck to help Clay get out of here, her filmy blue eyes clear and harden.

"No, Cassie," she tells me. "No."

Maynard is dismissive of Gran's reaction. "She loved Clay and wanted the best for him," he snaps. "We're leaving tomorrow, come hell or high water."

I don't push, because now that Clay is old enough to be more independent, Maynard gets stressed out by me still living with him. Gran and I, we're *a lot*. That's what he says when he's fed up.

Maynard is a pillar of the community, a deputy police chief, so his word carries weight around here. But that isn't enough to guarantee Clay a spot in the City.

Lady Luck must smile on my nephew for that.

In the living room, all my magazines are stacked in order. My precious parts are laid out in perfect lines, ready to be packed for our journey. A graphite filter sits next to a hunk of solar panel I salvaged from the town dump. I have screws, wires, nets, bits of metal, and a box of tools. I make sure to pack everything safely away before Maynard comes in. He hates it when I mess around trying to invent stuff, because then I have less time to clean and look after Gran.

But later, after I've read Clay a bedtime story and tucked him in, Maynard pulls me aside. "Do one more check of the house, Cassie. Make sure the engine and treads are good so we're ready to roll tomorrow."

I can't help but smile. He wouldn't have asked if he didn't trust my mechanical know-how. Maybe Lady Luck will smile upon me, too.

The morning of our departure dawns hot and bright, a reminder that fire season starts soon. Five years ago, everyone had to drive their houses to the town's auxiliary parking lot and hunker down to avoid a nearby blaze. That's the furthest I've ever traveled.

Until today.

I make a bet with Clay, wagering that he'll grow at least half a centimeter while we're gone. If he doesn't, he'll give me his best marble. If he does, I'll craft him a new toy.

He asks for an airplane, lips turning up in that amazing little smile of his. We rush to measure him against the doorframe once more, and then he heads to school, waving three times at the gate—once for each extra hug I gave him this morning.

I watch him until he's out of sight.

Maynard makes me pick the vegetables from our garden, even though it's too early. Half of them are severely underripe, but he says better us getting them than someone else. Then Maynard starts up the house's engine and we roll out toward the town's front gate.

I hang out a side window, a kind of freedom blowing through my hair. Even before Gran needed fulltime care, I didn't get out and about much. I was always the weird girl, the annoyance at the edges who broke the social rules over and over until it was better for me to stay out of sight, out of mind.

Sometimes it feels like I'm not really part of the community anymore, but maybe that's unavoidable in a town where people prize individualism above all.

Old Ulrich who guards the gates gives me a look I'm used to, somewhere between pity and contempt. His gaze flickers over Gran in her recliner. I watch uneasily as Ulrich's lips twist.

"May it be enough." Ulrich nods at Maynard and turns his gaze toward the distance again, watching for interlopers who might try to infiltrate the town, or steal our vegetables, or whatever interlopers do.

The gate shuts behind us, and we're truly on our way.

We drive west, watched with suspicion by the Ulrich-equivalents at each semi-identical town gate. On day four, we stop to repair one of the house's treads. Then our sewage filtration system breaks down, but with a little fiddling, I rig up a fix that'll hold us for the journey.

After two weeks of travel, the towns dwindle until we are surrounded by sere hills whose tan flanks guide us downward until we spot the ocean in the distance. I have never seen so much water in one place, except in pictures. But although the silvery-blue streak on the horizon is alluring, my eyes are drawn toward the jagged skyline of Tilt Town. At night, the town glows with a hellish flame from the pit on its outskirts, the depths burning endlessly. At school, we learned that's because of an unholy combination of natural gasses and whatever the Tilters throw down there. My classmate Paisley said they threw in babies, and the teacher didn't correct her.

"Aren't you happy I didn't ship your ass to the Tilters when you used to have all those tantrums over stupid crap like food textures and the wrong socks?" Maynard gestures to the wheel. "Take a shift. I need to stretch my legs."

As I sit, Maynard slams the reinforced door behind him. Because of his job, he got extra security features for his house, so the driver's capsule is wholly secure, like a commercial airplane's cockpit of old. Or a panic room.

Later that afternoon, I feed Gran from her favorite cup, but she turns her head at every spoonful. My worry turns into fear. She's growing weaker.

"Look," I whisper. "We're nearly to the ocean. In a few hours, we'll see Lady Luck."

Gran raises one bony hand in a weak signal, index finger extended. Maybe she's trying to sign Go, but her hand splays, and falls, and it turns into more of a No.

We arrive near sunset. Lady Luck towers above us, easily ten times as tall as Maynard. She stands knee-deep in ocean water, the tide lapping at her pearlescent marble skirts. One hand is upraised, as if to offer consecration. The other holds the leash of a giant stone dog, green-hued and brindled with salt. Lady Luck's thin lips press together, neither smiling nor frowning.

Yet.

I take a few careful steps onto the beach, searching the tideline for washed-up sacrifice. Maynard crunches past, leaving hard, deep footprints in the sand. He has a recent photograph of Clay, the one in which he's grinning so hard we can see two lost teeth. Maynard stops at the water's edge.

"See the dog?" he asks. "He and Luck always go hand in hand. He's called Hard Work. Kind of like you."

He laughs. I don't. I have a bad feeling in my stomach, and it isn't because I've been trying to eat the unripe vegetables from our garden.

"Maynard, what are you going to sacrifice?"

My brother kicks off his boots, rolls up his trousers, wades into the water. I want to do the same, to feel the luxury of liquid lapping around my toes, but I'm afraid of Maynard's stance, and especially of the vicious buck knife he's produced.

But I still trust him, don't I?

"Go inside, Cassie. Get Gran ready to move."

Habit makes me obey immediately. But halfway up the beach, I turn for a second look.

Maynard was the one who convinced Clay's mother to keep the baby inside her until full-term, even though pregnancy was killing her. It was a necessary sacrifice, Maynard said. Lady Luck smiled on Clay and took his mother in exchange. But surely Maynard doesn't mean to offer *himself* to the statue.

I pick up my pace. I rush indoors to shift Gran into her wheeled mobility chair. But she kicks, rocking perilously side to side, and I'm afraid she'll fall over—so I wedge her into the driver's capsule between the heavy door and the wall, where she's safest.

Then I crack open the window and watch Maynard wade up

to Lady Luck, to the tiny altar of her skirt.

"Here, have it all!" he shouts, and with movements I don't understand, he cuts the air nearby with a knife. A multi-colored aura hovers around the outline of his body, as if hesitating to leave.

"Take my dreams!" Maynard demands. "Take my ambitions!"

The aura coalesces and streams toward Lady Luck—a wonder of a moment, even if it isn't mine to experience. It reaches her marble in a riot of color and settles effervescently into her skirt folds before glowing upward.

When the light reaches her face, Maynard holds up the photo of Clay, and Lady Luck's stern lips lift into a smile focused at the boy.

I should be happy. This could be enough extra luck for Clay to get into the City. But I think, maybe once your own ambitions are all tied up in other folks, the only thing left to do is enforce them.

And Maynard doesn't look satisfied.

Sound carries near water, so I hear Maynard mutter, "Forgive me for what I'm about to do."

I realize, with a cold bolt of certainty, why the townsfolk averted their gazes as we rolled out of town. Why Ulrich pitied me at the gates. Maynard won't stop at giving up his own dreams and ambitions.

He'll sacrifice me and Gran, too.

I slam the capsule door shut. Jam my foot onto the pedal. We move at a crawl at first, but it's enough to soothe Gran's restlessness. She signs *go. Go. Go.*

Maynard's after us, sprinting up the beach, sunset glinting orange off his drawn knife.

I activate the fireproof panels. They creep slowly downward, shooting the house's fuel economy to hell. But we're already in hell, so what does it matter?

The weight of Maynard's body hitting the porch makes the house bounce on its treads. A warning light flashes on the dashboard as one of the panels halts.

My brother wrenches open the unlocked back door with a colossal bang.

He's already bellowing threats, storming his way to the driving area, fists bashing against metal. He's thwarted, furious, dangerous. A kind of fury stirs within me, too, something I haven't been allowed for years. I want the best for Clay. But not at the expense of my own dreams—or Gran's life.

I steer us uphill. Toward Tilt Town.

"Cassie!" Maynard bawls. "Come out right now!"

Defiance, long dormant, makes me crank the house's speed to maximum. At the door, Maynard's fists go ominously quiet. Footsteps creak down the hallway. They return faster than I'd like.

"Cassie," Maynard says more quietly. "I have an axe. Open up *now,* or you'll get hurt."

When I was Clay's age, Gran tried to teach me how to tell the difference between bluffing and truth.

"It's not safe to assume everyone means well," Gran said back when she could string sentences together coherently. "You're a vulnerable type, Cassie. You need to be able to sniff out a lie."

"Lies don't smell," I'd told her, and she'd looked up to the ceiling in despair. Then I'd gone back to my books and my inventions, neither of which are in the habit of being sneaky or untruthful.

Still, I didn't turn out completely naïve.

When I open the capsule door to Maynard, I'm armed with the flare gun he keeps underneath the driver's seat. Like a lot of things, it's a relic of a bygone time. But it'll scorch his face off if I shoot him at close range. Especially since he lied about the axe. He's only got a hatchet.

"You're not sacrificing Gran," I tell him. "Or me."

My brother scowls, but he backs away, moving to the side to let us pass as we reach the living room. I keep the gun pointed at his face as I bend to grab my box of personal possessions. I take a photo of Clay, too. Maynard sneers as I stow my stuff in the compartment underneath Gran's mobility chair.

"Your inventions and books won't keep you alive," my brother says. "Not in Tilt Town."

Maybe he's right. But there are worse fates.

I wheel Gran backward with one hand. Thump her over the threshold, past the slender lines of ink that show Clay's growth over the years. My throat is tight but my eyes are dry. I keep the flare gun pointed, even when the house begins to move again.

Maynard drives away, abandoning us at the side of the road as night descends.

I wheel Gran upward. There's nowhere else to go, so we head in the direction of Tilt Town.

This terrifies me, but if I was wrong about my brother, what else could I have been wrong about? Old aspirations stir at the edges of my mind like long-forgotten fever dreams. Maybe I could get a job, a *real* one—not just cleaning and looking after Clay and Gran.

I used to read job advertisements in the magazines that found their way to us. I'd narrow them down to what a town's education qualified me for. I wanted to be a research assistant. Anything above that required me to have been lucky enough for a college education. But Maynard told me I shouldn't apply. People like me talk wrong, act wrong, think wrong. I'd never fit in, so why bother?

The road is steep, and the night is moonless. Far behind, Lady Luck still glimmers with Maynard's sacrificed dreams. In the hills ahead, the pit casts its orange smolder against distant rooftops. The wheels on Gran's chair squeak until I have to hum under my breath to balance out the painful sound. There's no Maynard to scold me for making annoying noises.

But soon, I'm exhausted and dizzy, and Gran is moaning.

I push us onto the road's shoulder and lift Gran from her chair, making sure her head doesn't droop forward and block off her windpipe. We sink to the ground and I cradle her to me. She is so weak. Even when I explain what's going on, she only twirls my hair gently, in a movement that's somehow both a baby's questing hand and a mother's soothing touch.

There's no point fearing the unknown when death is already in my lap. The chill of the night keeps me from sleeping soundly, but I drop into an occasional doze.

When dawn breaks and I shudder awake for the final time,

Gran is dead in my arms, and there's a group of Tilters staring down at us.

Grief numbs my fear. I cannot speak. All I can do is hold Gran's cooling hand.

The Tilters don't look like devils or rapists, like Maynard used to call them. They wear homespun clothes and concerned expressions, and when they help lift Gran's body into her chair, they're gentle. We walk slowly into Tilt Town. I keep hold of Gran's hand, half-expecting it to rise to sign for water, or food, or warmth. It stays still, no matter how I cling.

I'm homeless. No more Gran, no more Clay. I have to recalibrate. But how?

Tilt Town's steep streets and stationary dwellings prove less threatening than I expect. People eye me curiously from doorsteps, but don't ask prying questions. There's no Ulrich equivalent to interrogate me, because there are no gates here.

I still can't talk, so eventually, people call on someone named Big Joan.

"Come on," Big Joan says, brooking no argument. She grasps Gran's chair with hands twice the size of mine, and I follow her broad shoulders toward her residence: a trio of shipping containers loosely welded together. A ramp leads to her living room. Poorly-made pipes run the length of the room, connecting to the bathroom at the far end.

Big Joan pours me half a cup of water through an extremely inefficient filter.

"We get all sorts here, but most of them aren't dead on arrival," the woman tells me in a gruff contralto. "I know you're in shock, but we gotta find a resting place for your loved one. Usually, folks opt to be recycled. Helps crops. Helps others live. Now and then, we get those who wanna be burned or put to the ocean. So, you decide which she would have wanted while I leave you be for a bit."

Big Joan exits the room. While I think about Gran's next steps, I reach for the filter. I have to keep my fingers busy. When I was a kid, I used to break things apart one bit at a time, until Gran gave me tools of my own. Then I turned destroying into fixing.

Tears blur my eyes as I lean past Gran to fetch my box of stuff. I need a focus, or I'll drown in grief. I mend the handle of the portable filter and shore up the gaping left side, where microplastics could leak through. By the time Big Joan returns, I'm wedged under her sink, checking out the house's rudimentary filtration system, which has major problems.

My fingers explore. My brain calms. Big Joan waits.

"Gran would want to be recycled," I say when I recover the ability to speak. "She always tried to teach us to help others."

"What's your name?" Big Joan asks on the second day.

We sit in front of her living room container, our feet propped in the street. Tilters pass by, and each one nods to us. They don't keep themselves to themselves here.

I lift my eyes. The town's arable land lies in the mid distance. Gran's body will contribute to the crops grown there. I remain silent for a few beats, considering Big Joan's question. I don't feel like who I used to be.

"Cass," I finally say.

An hour ago, I finished my repairs on Big Joan's house, and now there is no more risk of cross-contamination when the house recycles waste. Previously, she'd had been at high risk of dysentery or cholera. Her filtration system still isn't perfect, but it's much safer.

Fixing it kept me busy, but dread settles across my shoulders, weighing me down until I'm surprised the chair I'm perched on doesn't snap into hundreds of plastic shards. Big Joan told me she often takes in newcomers for a day or two, just until they get on their feet. Now it's time for her to thank me for my work and send me on my way. To where, I don't know. I'm too numb to panic. Probably, I'll find a spot nearby and wait to join Gran. Maynard was right. I have no clue how to live independently.

Then Big Joan speaks, and the chair doesn't break, and everything in me is suddenly light.

"You're good at fixing things, and I'm not. I'd like you to stay with me, Cass," she says. "For as long as you want."

Living with Big Joan gives me the luxury of my own time and space. The Tilters quickly get into the habit of bringing me City trash, which I occasionally turn into useful treasure.

Water is scarce, but the situation is worse here, because the shortage is exacerbated by position. Any rain the Tilters gets runs swiftly down to the City. I wander between propped-up dwellings and make notes on gradients and groundwater and revel in the fact that people here don't interrupt my focus by demanding to know what I'm doing, is the house clean, and what's for supper?

People here constantly rebuild, rejig, reshuffle. In the first month, the ground tilts three times. The movement is somehow both subtle and sudden. One moment, everything is normal. Then, without even seeming to move, the hill slants an extra quarter of a centimeter away from the City—as if the place is weighing down the world, making Tilt Town rise to precarious heights. The pit shifts ever-closer, throwing its light over everything.

At night, from the new balcony I welded to Big Joan's upper level, I often stare in Lady Luck's direction. When she glows from recent sacrifice, she lights distant pale walls, lending the City an extra moon's worth of gentle whiteness. At times like that, her shadow falls across Tilt Town, dampening the constant orange glow of the pit. It's an uneasy darkness, layered like a series of bloodstains seen only under UV light.

Seasons pass. I wouldn't bother to count them if it weren't for Clay.

By now, he's twelve. When one of the Tilters manages to acquire premium internet, we crowd around a screen and carve up the time into precious minutes. One day, my curiosity becomes too much, and I make myself join in. My fingers fly over the keyboard. Clay's name pops up almost immediately.

Maynard's sacrifice was enough. Lady Luck got Clay a spot at a moderately prestigious City school. I move away from the screen, wracked with relief, with guilt, even with jealousy—but above all, I just miss my nephew.

He would have grown that half a centimeter by now. In my spare time, I craft him the airplane I'd promised. Not a flimsy toy, but a display model fit for the teenager he'll soon become. Maynard always wanted him to like fighter jets or bombers, but Clay's most treasured models were of commercial airplanes. When I finish, I carve the name of his favorite airline and flight number—one of the last ever flown—into the metal.

Then I wrap it carefully and Big Joan arranges for it to be delivered to his school in the City.

"Do you think he'll like it?" I ask her.

"No point wondering," she says from the kitchen, where she's fixing up a batch of soup for a communal lunch. "You did as much as you have control over."

Big Joan has people skills but not a ton of book smarts, and I'm basically the opposite. What we have, I tell her, is a symbiotic relationship, and she always makes sure to acknowledge observations like that with a serious nod before asking me if I've remembered to stay hydrated. I'm glad for her skills as I help carry bowls and utensils.

Today, we watch the news. Towns like my old one have begun developing slants of their own. There's lots of talk about how to brace treads and build stronger gates.

It's not a disaster yet, the talking heads claim. With enough sacrifice, Lady Luck will smile upon their own. Look at the City, they say. It's slowly sinking, but they're coping.

We'll cope too, right?

Except we don't.

Even my newest inventions cannot get Tilt Town enough water. It hasn't rained more than a few drops for months. We're all going thirsty and unwashed. I've done everything possible: maximized the efficiency of each wastewater system, rigged up extra nets to collect fog and dew, and set my solar desalinization stations to work overtime processing oceanwater.

We don't have enough resources to collect our most-needed resource.

What hurts the most is the way people look at me as if *I* can fix this. In despair one night, I climb to the top of Big Joan's roof with my telescope. Colonizing Mars is a ship that's long since sailed, but watching stars reminds me that the universe is composed of more than just us and the City.

After a long time peering through a homemade telescope, I make out lights that aren't stars. I frown, adjust lenses, and continue observation. The lights turn out to be small, state-of-the-art drones. They circle far above, a glittering, fine mesh stretching between them.

No wonder we're not getting any water. The City is stealing our rain before it even reaches us.

We'll all die if we don't figure out how to change this.

Big Joan calls a meeting. Everyone in Tilt Town comes.

There's an energy that flows in most humans, one that seems to be several parts sectarianism mixed with a large dash of magical thinking and a varying dose of self-preservation. When I announce that we've reached a tipping point, I expect resource-hoarding to commence and for me to be considered a burden again.

But nobody here is overly interested in maintaining the status quo.

So when I'm done explaining, everyone stays quiet. Even stranger, they look to me for a plan.

"I've thought a lot about seesaws," I tell everyone haltingly, encouraged by the way Big Joan stands at my shoulder. "They're logical, but they also taught me about human nature. When you're light, and a heavy kid climbs onto the other side, they might fling you toward the stratosphere. That's what the City's doing. Maybe they don't set out to do it, but it's happening anyway."

"Then what do we do?" a person shouts from the crowd, which has swollen to a size I never expected. We've gotten more town refugees lately.

"What *can* we do?" someone else mutters. "They can steal

anything they like and call it their due."

Big Joan steps forward before things get frayed. She thumps a fist against her heart.

"Everyone's got something in them that helps a community. But they aren't always given a chance to show it."

People nod and shuffle at her words. This buys me time to talk about my calculations of force and mass. I arm the crowd with hard numbers, and then I tell them, flat out, the only thing that'll fix this situation.

"It's time to kill Lady Luck."

We march toward the ocean, carrying what we need to topple the phenomenon that killed my parents and saved my nephew. I think of Clay a lot these days. I'm not one for magical thinking, but I choose to believe he got the airplane I sent. That he knows I'm still alive. That I love him.

Lady Luck stands thigh-deep in the water when we arrive, her skirts red with recent sacrifice. As a final act of self-preservation, she smiles upon me, and whispers into my mind that the City wants me, has *always* wanted me, I'm so smart, I'm so *incredibly* useful—but I'm done with Lady Luck's foibles.

I gesture, and the Tilters come forward.

We haul Lady Luck off her pedestal, and the tenuous link between the statue and her dog breaks forever. The canine representation of Hard Work stands alone in the swelling tide as we drag Lady Luck up the steep hill, toward the glowing pit beyond. We're sending her to hell.

By the time we reach the halfway point, we're sweating and trembling with exertion. Lady Luck tries to work her magic on the hundreds of Tilters at her ropes. *It could be you*, she whispers in increasing desperation.

"Statistically improbable!" I take to shouting. A few take up the words, like a rallying cry. Others snap back with their own rejoinders.

"It's *never* people like me," my neighbor bellows, thumping marble with a walking aid.

"It should be all of us!" another person yells.

"No more sacrifice!" Big Joan puts her back into pulling.

The pit's foul miasma hits us, and our breaths turn shallow. The fires below are fueled by City garbage and natural gasses, not Tilter babies like my classmate once claimed. We heave once more. Marble flashes.

A deep groan shudders through the earth as Lady Luck falls headfirst into orange flames.

Lady Luck is dead, and everything changes.

The land underneath Tilt Town begins to sink, levelling out with the City. Because the Tilters are so used to working as a community, we're quick to save our dwellings. Big Joan rushes from place to place, only pausing when we see what's happening to the walls over which Luck once smiled.

They shift, slowly but surely. The City's foundations were never built on level ground to begin with, so its walls sag quickly to one side. People put their hands atop shoulders of children, pointing, saying: *you may never see this again in your lifetime.*

I know this is right, and I also know this is wrong. Like a seesaw unweighted, the earth underfoot continues to settle, and my thoughts turn to Clay. My sweet nephew with his quick smile. If I hadn't had his growth to cherish alongside Gran's slow deterioration and Maynard's hard words, how would I have managed to keep my own balance for so long?

One Tilter sets up a projector and begins streaming footage. For the City, the world has flipped sideways. Walls are floors and floors are walls, and the gates stand wide open to the outside for the first time in centuries. I clench my hands into fists as I watch people run for their lives. I lean in close to the screen. Searching. Hoping. A drone camera zooms in on a group of students rushing toward the gates. They're nearly there when a chunk of masonry smashes into their midst. The frontrunners are unscathed, but one of their fellows is trapped, legs waving, screaming for help. My stomach twists.

A sudden patter of rain cuts through our silence. The City's drones have fallen, and people turn away from the screened drama, scurrying outside with their mouths open, salt-encrusted faces turned to a new sky as stolen, hoarded water falls in fat drops.

But I stay with the projector. Pause it. Rewind. Back to the falling masonry. Back to one student in particular, whose escape was narrow, almost miraculous.

I see the whites of his eyes underneath dark, curly hair. No bag or other possessions. Only a battered model airplane clutched in one hand.

I watch the brief footage over and over. I study the stoop of his shoulders, the direction of his gaze, the bend of his legs, the quick flex of his arm as he turns to look at his fallen fellow. Will he stay and help, or keep running?

The camera cuts away at the crucial point of Clay's decision.

I rewind, but Big Joan touches my shoulder before I can hit play again.

"Let's travel down to the gates together," she says, "so we can aid whoever makes it out."

Kat Murray is a neurodivergent writer from the San Francisco Bay Area. She spent her early childhood in a counterculture community aboard a boat, and now lives in London with her husband and two children. She has a BA in Journalism from San Francisco State University. When she isn't writing, she's probably gaming, in a forest, or making a cup of tea.

The Last Great Repair Tech of the American Midwest

Ellis Nye

Wendy "Darling" Marszałek

It is with sorrow that this paper announces the passing of one of our town's greatest treasures, Wendy "Darling" Marszałek. She died on August 18th, 2081, in her early eighties. Contrary to her frequent predictions, she did not die "crushed under a pile of old tech"; she went peacefully, in her sleep, at her home here in Adden, MO, just a few miles from where she was born. I'm afraid I don't know her exact birth date, since she never told it to me, and there's no one else to ask. I only know that she was born here in town because she pointed the old hospital building out to me once, when she was giving me a tour of Adden. (She was shocked that no one had done so right when I moved in, and never seemed to understand that it was because there wasn't much of the town *to* tour.)

Wendy was predeceased by most of her family and close friends; she never married or had kids, and her older sister, Leah, passed in the heat wave of 2072. As far as anyone knows, Wendy's great-nephew, Rupert, is alive, but I was unable to contact him. After asking around town, I've realized I may be Wendy's closest living friend, so I volunteered to take on the obituary, even though I'm just the paper's photographer and illustrator. (If there's an afterlife, Wendy is out there boasting right now that a real newspaper reporter wrote *her* obituary, ignoring the fact that I'm not a writer at all.)

I don't know how to sum Wendy up, and I feel like there were whole parts of her personality I never got to see. Here are a few things I can tell you about her. Wendy's house was always a cluttered mess, filled with broken machines, except for her kitchen. Her kitchen she kept spotless, and once a week she'd devote a whole day to covering her counters in dumpling-making materials. She would then eat almost nothing but those dumplings for the rest of the week, until it was time to make more. Wendy tried a different dumpling recipe from a different culture every time, and I never noticed her repeating one.

Wendy always wore steel-toed boots, and she walked with a slight limp. She said the two were connected, but refused to explain why.

She was the Grand Marshal of the Adden pride parade a total of eleven times—five of them in a row. It was the only time I saw her out of her usual uniform of jeans and a T-shirt, wearing a sharp, custom-made boiler suit sewn in the trans flag colors instead.

Wendy loved to sing while she was working, and she was absolutely terrible at it. One time when she was working on my fridge, it got so bad I had to leave the house.

She was a regular at the town dump, and after a few half-hearted attempts to keep her from trespassing, they just gave up and told her to come by whenever she wanted. She had a great eye for things that could be salvaged, and would rant at length about how people throw everything out, because, "No one knows how to fix anything these days!" She would, however, be the first to admit that no one knows how to fix anything these days because almost nothing's worth fixing, and most people figure you might as well try to find a new one somewhere.

One time I was walking past her house and heard an explosion; when I looked in to see what had happened, her entire kitchen was covered in her best attempt at homemade wine. She was also covered in it, and when she saw me in the doorway (she never bothered to lock her door) she licked the wine off her lips and said it tasted like shit. I got a bottle of wine from her, labeled "Shit Wine", for my birthday the next year. It did taste like shit.

Everyone here in Adden has at least one "Wendy story", so I asked around to get an idea of what to include. I found that just about all of them were a lot like my own experiences, so I thought I would tell all of our readers my own Wendy story.

Sometime in September of 2068, two of our remaining three computers at the paper went out. I don't remember what problem the desktop was having, but the laptop was acting like it was haunted; the cursor would move on its own, and half the keys on the keyboard didn't work anymore. As the writers were all busy, and I had some free time, I was tasked with fixing both computers. The internet had been down all that week, and I'm not tech-savvy myself, so I was beating my head against the wall as I restarted them for a third time, hoping that it would magically change something. Then, like a 5'2" vision of an angel in a pair of dirty jeans, Wendy appeared.

I think I just started crying at her, but clearly she picked out enough words in between the blubbering to figure out what was going on. She sat down at the desktop computer, worked some kind of magic, and told me that it was a loss. I started panicking, because we'd been using some knockoff graphic design software to set up the newspaper pages on the desktop—it was the only computer we had left with the power to run the software—and the then twice-a-week paper was supposed to go to print in a few hours. Wendy somehow managed to get the pages off the desktop in a usable file format so we could transfer them to the laptop (which she kept limping along for another year and a half) and we could print the paper.

After that, we here at the newspaper saw a lot more of Wendy. With the desktop out of commission, we had to start getting creative. Luckily, we had this huge old monstrosity of a copy machine that must have been used for something industrial, so we were able to write up articles on the laptop and the tablet, print them out, and glue them to one of the newspaper sheets to make copies to distribute. The laptop and the tablet were much more fragile than the desktop had ever been, and like I said, the laptop gave up the ghost a year and a half later, with Wendy coming in almost every day to nurse it.

"You need to start planning ahead," she told me on one of those days; she often did that, starting in the middle of a conversation. "For when you don't have computers anymore." I had thought about that, briefly, but it was overwhelming; I've never been techy and I don't know where to start. Everyone else at the paper seemed so busy—this was just before I switched over to illustrating articles and became just as busy as the rest of them—and I hadn't brought it up. Plus, part of me still believed that we could buy new ones that would actually work, instead of breaking down within a few months.

I gaped at Wendy like a fish out of water. "I'll get you some typewriters," she said. She eyed our copy machine critically.

"And a replacement for that, in the next few years. After that, I'll have to start asking people to break into museums for the *old* machines."

That's how all the Wendy stories I heard went; she figured out what you needed long before you did. She was a genius at repairing a wide variety of technology ("Except sewing machines, they hate me and the feeling's mutual"), and if she didn't know how to fix it, she knew someone who could. Dee Herrera used to live down the street from Wendy. She's diabetic, and had always found that a somewhat outdated insulin pump worked best for her needs. Well, about twenty years ago, the company that made that pump announced that they would no longer be supporting it or offering repairs; everyone would just have to upgrade. The upgraded pumps would get the finest customer support the company had, naturally, and whenever they broke they would immediately be replaced with the newest model. Which was exactly what Dee *didn't* want. Wendy heard Dee fretting about this at a neighborhood party, and before Dee knew it, Wendy had gotten her in contact with an organization of hackers—many diabetic themselves—who were working on keeping that pump model running without the company's support. Today, Dee uses a new and improved version that was designed by one of those original hackers to mimic her old, discontinued one. If she ever has a problem with it, she can ask a real person what to do, and they'll give her multiple solutions as soon as they get her message. It's not an exaggeration, Dee told me, to say that Wendy saved her life.

I can't possibly list every story that people told me about Wendy, but here are a few people whose lives she touched:

Álvaro Garret, whose severe asthma forces him to stay indoors for the entirety of the dust season, relying on consistent air filtration to keep his environment safe.

Melania Okafor, who needed to keep her ancient computer working so she could stay in touch with her far-flung family.

Leo Tong, the owner of the only restaurant in town, The Bluebird. We're all very thankful that Wendy kept his kitchen appliances working for so long, and that she was able to find replacements for him when they finally died.

Aiden Wise, whose powerchair broke down in the middle of the sidewalk one day. Luckily, Wendy was just stepping out of the barbershop next door.

Coral Ojeda, who works two towns over, and who refused to get a new car since it would just break down in two years anyway. Wendy kept hers kicking for almost twenty years, and only stopped because Coral got a job in town that she could walk to.

And, of course, myself, and the entire newspaper staff. I think Wendy would be delighted to note that I am currently typing this obituary—after hand-writing it out—on one of the typewriters she procured for the newspaper. At this point, we do all our writing on a pair of solid, old-fashioned typewriters that are older than some of the newspaper employees. (Myself included.) They break down far less than the computers ever did, and with the new copier set up, we're more efficient than ever.

Even from beyond the grave, Wendy is helping us with a problem that we'd barely started to consider. She was meticulous about keeping her will up-to-date, and I wasn't surprised to hear that I was in it. Wendy left me a few interesting gadgets, as well as a slip of paper. On it is the contact information for a friend of hers who might know where to obtain some historical newspaper printing machines. "Just in case," Wendy wrote.

—Peter Lamarr

Ellis Nye (any pronouns) is a scientist, fiber artist, and writer. Ze lives in New England, and wrote this short story on a laptop that the tech support people wanted to throw away because it was “too hard to fix”. That was three years ago.

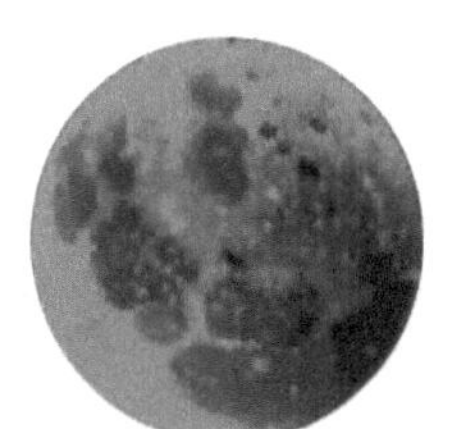

www.ingramcontent.com/pod-product-compliance
Lightning Source LLC
Chambersburg PA
CBHW020753190726
48285CB00006B/2004

* 9 7 8 1 9 5 5 3 6 0 1 1 1 *